Oxford Secondary English

Book 1

John Seely

and
Frank Ash
Frank Green
Chris Woodhead

Oxford
University
Press

Oxford University Press, Walton Street, Oxford OX2 6DP

Oxford New York Toronto
Delhi Bombay Calcutta Madras Karachi
Petaling Jaya Singapore Hong Kong Tokyo
Nairobi Dar es Salaam Cape Town
Melbourne Auckland

and associated companies in
Berlin Ibadan

Oxford is a trade mark of Oxford University Press

© Oxford University Press 1982

First published 1982
Reprinted 1982, 1983 (twice), 1984, 1985, 1986, 1987, 1988,
         1989, 1990, 1991

ISBN 0 19 831133 8

There is a pupil's book and a teacher's book for each
year of *Oxford Secondary English*. The teacher's
book is an integral part of the course and contains
reproducible assignments on the material in the
pupil's book. Notes and advice for the teacher are
also included.

Printed in Great Britain by
Thomson Litho Ltd, East Kilbride, Scotland

Contents

What does this machine do?
How does it work?
Just suppose you could invent *any* machine;
what would you design yours to do?
Just suppose men came to depend too
much on machines . . .

Just Suppose...

Just suppose you were a hero . . .

The Fashists★ had gone to ground behind the banking in the field on the far side of the playground. They maintained a sporadic fire from behind their cover and there was an occasional tinkle of breaking glass as another window pane shattered in the bullet-scarred south wing of the school. Joby and his fellow defenders relaxed below the level of the windows, resting after cutting down repeated enemy assaults across the open stretch of tarmac. Elsa sat on the floor beside Joby, tired from the continuous loading and reloading of the rifles which had burned hot in Joby's hands. Joby smiled at her and touched her hand reassuringly.

'Don't worry: there'll be help coming soon.'

The relief column was on its way from Pontefract Barracks. Mr Morrison had got a message through before the telephone lines were cut.

'I'm not afraid,' Elsa told him. 'Not with you here. I think you're so brave, Joby.'

Joby shrugged. 'I'm only doing my duty.'

She gave him a smile that melted his heart as the headmaster came crawling on his hands and knees along the line of defenders.

'Everything all right here?' he said as he reached Joby and Elsa.

'All in order, sir,' Joby answered.

'Good, good. You're all doing a magnificent job.' Mr Morrison raised his head carefully so that he could see out. 'Well, we seem to have given them something they won't forget in a hurry. I doubt if they'll try another assault now.' He stopped and started. 'Good lord, look!'

Joby lifted himself up, rifle at the ready. A soldier had clambered over the rim of the banking and was now breaking into a run across the open playground, coming towards the school with a small round object in his right hand.

'It's a hand grenade!' the headmaster cried, and Joby said calmly:

'Leave him to me, sir.'

He had the soldier in his sights already, the rifle barrel resting on the window-ledge and turning slightly as it followed the running figure. He waited deliberately until the soldier halted, drew the pin from the grenade and swung back his arm for the throw. Then Joby shot him, the impact of the bullet spinning the man off his feet as the

★ Fashists = Fascists, a name once given to the Germans and Italians during the Second World War.

grenade exploded and blew shattered lumps of tarmac into the air.

'Good shot, Joby!' the headmaster cried and Joby, his rifle covering the edge of the field for signs of further movement, said briefly:

'It was nothing, sir.'

Elsa's eyes were turned up to him, glowing with admiration.

He became aware that somebody was talking to him.

'What?' He looked at the dark-smocked barber standing over him.

'I said, do you want your hair cutting or are you just going to sit there all morning?'

Joby said, 'Oh, sorry,' and got up and walked across to the empty chair.

'You were miles away just then, weren't you?' Mr Manley, the barber, said as he shook the sheet, swung it round Joby in a practised sweep and tucked the edge into his collar.

'I was just thinking about something.'

Stan Barstow, *Joby*

Questions to think and talk about	1 Do you ever daydream like this?
	2 Are daydreams just a silly waste of time?
	3 Could they ever be useful? Or dangerous?
	4 What kind of person does Joby dream that he is?
	5 Who do you dream of being, or what do you dream of doing?
Writing	1 Write a story about your own daydreams.
	2 Complete this title and then write about it:
	If I were . . . . . .

Just suppose you won £25,000 . . .

Just enter this simple competition and you could win £25,000 worth of holidays or sports equipment and training. It's simple! Which of the foods listed do 11 year olds like best? What comes next? Place the foods in order of popularity from 1 to 6. Then complete the sentence on the Entry Form.

Foods
A   steak and kidney pudding
B   baked beans on toast
C   fish and chips
D   roast beef and Yorkshire pudding
E   bacon and egg
F   Irish stew

Entry Form

Against each figure write down *the letter only* of the food that you think should go there.

1

2

3

4

5

6

Complete this sentence by adding not more than fifteen words:

My favourite food is ....*because*

....

....

NAME AND ADDRESS:

Send your entry to:
Great Universal Food Factories, Western Avenue, Slough.

Writing   Write your entry for the competition.

G

GREAT UNIVERSAL FOOD FACTORIES, WESTERN AVENUE, SLOUGH

Dear ....,

I am writing to tell you the good news that you have won first prize in our Great Grub ! competition. As you know, the prize is worth £25,000. But there are some conditions. I should be grateful if you would read them very carefully.

Before you receive the prize, you must send G.U.F.F. a declaration signed by your parents, saying that your competition entry was your own unaided work. You must then agree to take part in two television commercials, advertising G.U.F.F. products.

The prize will not be given as cash, but as credits with selected firms – according to which prize you choose. If you choose the holiday, then the money must be spent as follows:

travel: £7,500
accommodation: £10,000
excursions: £3,000
clothing: £2,000
equipment: £2,500

If you choose the sports prize, the money must be spent as follows:

coaching and advice: £8,000
facilities (booking courts etc.): £2,000
travel and tickets to see matches and competitions: £5,000
clothing: £4,000
equipment: £6,000

In either case you are allowed to share the prize with one friend or relative.

Finally, I must receive from you, within one week, a letter giving me full details of how you plan to use your prize. I look forward to hearing from you.

Yours sincerely,

A J Poston

A.J. Poston, Managing Director, G.U.F.F.

Writing   Write your answer to Mr Poston.

Thinking

I may be silent, but
I'm thinking.
I may not talk, but
Don't mistake me for a wall.

Tsuboi Shigeji

Alone

I'm alone in the evening
when the family sits
reading and sleeping
and I watch the fire in close
to see flame goblins
wriggling out of their caves
for the evening.

Later I'm alone
when the bath has gone cold around me
and I have put my foot
beneath the cold tap
where it can dribble
through valleys between my toes
out across the white plain of my foot
and bibble bibble into the sea.

I'm alone
when mum's switched out the light
my head against the pillow
listening to ca thump ca thump
in the middle of my ears.
It's my heart.

Michael Rosen

Just suppose there was no more TV . . . .

The most important thing we've learned,
So far as children are concerned,
Is never, NEVER, NEVER let
Them near your television set –
Or better still, just don't install
The idiotic thing at all.
In almost every house we've been,
We've watched them gaping at the screen.
They loll and slop and lounge about,
And stare until their eyes pop out.
(Last week in someone's place we saw
A dozen eyeballs on the floor.)
They sit and stare and stare and sit
Until they're hypnotized by it,
Until they're absolutely drunk
With all that shocking ghastly junk.
Oh yes, we know it keeps them still,
They don't climb out the window sill,
They never fight or kick or punch,
They leave you free to cook the lunch
And wash the dishes in the sink –
But did you ever stop to think,
To wonder just exactly what
This does to your beloved tot?
IT ROTS THE SENSES IN THE HEAD!
IT KILLS IMAGINATION DEAD!
IT CLOGS AND CLUTTERS UP THE MIND!
IT MAKES A CHILD SO DULL AND BLIND
HE CAN NO LONGER UNDERSTAND
A FANTASY, A FAIRYLAND!
HIS BRAIN BECOMES AS SOFT AS CHEESE!
HIS POWERS OF THINKING RUST AND FREEZE!
HE CANNOT THINK – HE ONLY SEES!
'All right!' you'll cry, 'All right!' you'll
say,
'But if we take the set away,
What shall we do to entertain
Our darling children! Please explain!'
We'll answer this by asking you,
'What used the darling ones to do?
How used they keep themselves contented
Before this monster was invented?'
Have you forgotten? Don't you know?
We'll say it very loud and slow:

THEY . . . USED . . . TO . . . READ! They'd READ and READ,
AND READ and READ, and then proceed
To READ some more. Great Scott! Gadzooks!
One half their lives was reading books!
The nursery shelves held books galore!
Books cluttered up the nursery floor!
And in the bedroom, by the bed,
More books were waiting to be read!
Such wondrous, fine, fantastic tales
Of dragons, gypsies, queens, and whales
And treasure isles, and distant shores
Where smugglers rowed with muffled oars,
And pirates wearing purple pants,
And sailing ships and elephants,
And cannibals crouching round the pot,
Stirring away at something hot.
(It smells so good, what can it be?
Good gracious, it's Penelope.)
The younger ones had Beatrix Potter
With Mr Tod, the dirty rotter,
And Squirrel Nutkin, Pigling Bland,
And Mrs Tiggy-Winkle and –
Just How The Camel Got His Hump,
And How The Monkey Lost His Rump,
And Mr Toad, and bless my soul,
There's Mr Rat and Mr Mole –
Oh, books, what books they used to know,
Those children living long ago!
So please, oh please, we beg, we pray,
Go throw your TV set away,
And in its place you can install
A lovely bookshelf on the wall.
Then fill the shelves with lots of books,
Ignoring all the dirty looks,
The screams and yells, the bites and kicks,
And children hitting you with sticks –
Fear not, because we promise you
That, in about a week or two
Of having nothing else to do,
They'll now begin to feel the need
Of having something good to read.
And once they start – oh boy, oh boy!
You watch the slowly growing joy
That fills their hearts. They'll grow so keen
They'll wonder what they'd ever seen
In that ridiculous machine,
That nauseating, foul, unclean,
Repulsive television screen!
And later, each and every kid
Will love you more for what you did.

Roald Dahl, *Charlie and the Chocolate Factory*

Just suppose it was the last night of the world . . .

'What would you do if you knew that this was the last night of the world?'

'What would I do? You mean seriously?'

'Yes, seriously.'

'I don't know. I hadn't thought.'

He poured some coffee. In the background the two girls were playing blocks on the parlour rug in the light of the green hurricane lamps. There was an easy, clean aroma of the brewed coffee in the evening air.

'Well, better start thinking about it,' he said.

'You don't mean it!'

He nodded.

'A war?'

He shook his head.

'Not the hydrogen or atom bomb?'

'No.'

'Or germ warfare?'

'None of those at all,' he said, stirring his coffee slowly. 'But just, let's say, the closing of a book.'

'I don't think I understand.'

'No, nor do I, really; it's just a feeling. Sometimes it frightens me, sometimes I'm not frightened at all but at peace.' He glanced in at the girls and their yellow hair shining in the lamplight. 'I didn't say anything to you. It first happened about four nights ago.'

'What?'

'A dream I had. I dreamed that it was all going to be over, and a voice said it was; not any kind of voice I can remember, but a voice anyway, and it said things would stop here on Earth. I didn't think too much about it the next day, but then I went to the office and caught Stan Willis looking out the window in the middle of the afternoon, and I said a penny for your thoughts, Stan, and he said, I had a dream last night, and before he even told me the dream I knew what it was. I could have told him, but he told me and I listened to him.'

'It was the same dream?'

'The same. I told Stan I had dreamed it too. He didn't seem surprised. He relaxed, in fact. Then we started walking through the office, for the hell of it. It wasn't planned. We didn't say, "Let's walk around." We just walked on our own, and everywhere we saw

40 people looking at their desks or their hands or out windows. I talked to a few. So did Stan.'

'And they all had dreamed?'

'All of them. The same dream, with no difference.'

'Do you believe in it?'

45 'Yes. I've never been more certain.'

'And when will it stop? The world, I mean.'

'Sometime during the night for us, and then as the night goes on around the world, that'll go too. It'll take twenty-four hours for it all to go.'

50 They sat awhile not touching their coffee. Then they lifted it slowly and drank, looking at each other.

'Do we deserve this?' she said.

'It's not a matter of deserving; it's just that things didn't work out. I notice you didn't even argue about this. Why not?'

55 'I guess I've a reason,' she said.

'The same one everyone at the office had?'

She nodded slowly. 'I didn't want to say anything. It happened last night. And the women on the block talked about it, among themselves, today. They dreamed. I thought it was only a

60 coincidence.' She picked up the evening paper. 'There's nothing in the paper about it.'

'Everyone knows, so there's no need.'

He sat back in his chair, watching her. 'Are you afraid?'

Ray Bradbury, *The Illustrated Man*

Just suppose you started to shrink . . .

Something very strange was happening to Treehorn.

The first thing he noticed was that he couldn't reach the shelf in his closet that he had always been able to reach before, the one where he hid his candy bars and bubble gum.

Then he noticed that his clothes were getting too big.

'My trousers are all stretching or something,' said Treehorn to his mother. 'I'm tripping on them all the time.'

'That's too bad, dear,' said his mother, looking into the oven. 'I do hope this cake isn't going to fall,' she said.

'And my sleeves come down way below my hands,' said Treehorn. 'So my shirts must be stretching, too.'

'Think of that,' said Treehorn's mother. 'I just don't know why this cake isn't rising the way it should. Mrs Abernale's cakes are *always* nice. They *always* rise.'

Treehorn started out of the kitchen. He tripped on his trousers, which indeed did seem to be getting longer and longer.

At dinner that night Treehorn's father said, 'Do sit up, Treehorn. I can hardly see your head.'

'I *am* sitting up,' said Treehorn. 'This is as far up as I come. I think I must be shrinking or something.'

'I'm sorry my cake didn't turn out very well,' said Treehorn's mother.

'It's very nice, dear,' said Treehorn's father politely.

By this time Treehorn could hardly see over the top of the table.

'Sit up, dear,' said Treehorn's mother.

'I *am* sitting up,' said Treehorn. 'It's just that I'm shrinking.'

'What, dear?' asked his mother.

'I'm shrinking. Getting smaller,' said Treehorn.

'If you want to pretend you're shrinking, that's all right,' said Treehorn's mother,' as long as you don't do it at the table.'

'But I *am* shrinking,' said Treehorn.

'Don't argue with your mother,' said Treehorn's father.

'He does look a little smaller,' said Treehorn's mother, looking at Treehorn. 'Maybe he *is* shrinking.'

'Nobody shrinks,' said Treehorn's father.

'Well, I'm shrinking,' said Treehorn. 'Look at me.'

Treehorn's father looked at Treehorn.

'Why, you're shrinking,' said Treehorn's father. 'Look, Emily,

Treehorn is shrinking. He's much smaller than he used to be.'

'Oh dear,' said Treehorn's mother. 'First it was the cake, and now it's this. Everything happens at once.'

At school the next day

When he went into class, his teacher said, 'Nursery school is down at the end of the school, honey.'

'I'm Treehorn' said Treehorn.

'If you're Treehorn, why are you so small?' asked the teacher.

'Because I'm shrinking,' said Treehorn. 'I'm getting smaller.'
'Well, I'll let it go for today,' said his teacher. 'But see that it's taken care of before tomorrow. We don't shrink in this class.'

After recess, Treehorn was thirsty, so he went down the hall to the water bubbler. He couldn't reach it, and he tried to jump up. He still couldn't get a drink, but he kept jumping up and down, trying.

His teacher walked by. 'Why, Treehorn,' she said. 'That isn't like you, jumping up and down in the hall. Just because you're shrinking, it does not mean you have special privileges. What if all the children in the *school* started jumping up and down in the halls? I'm afraid you'll have to go to the Principal's office, Treehorn.'

So Treehorn went to the Principal's office.

'I'm supposed to see the Principal,' said Treehorn to the lady in the Principal's outer office.

'It's a very busy day,' said the lady. 'Please check here on this form the reason you have to see him. That will save time. Be sure to put your name down, too. That will save time. And write clearly. That will save time.'

Treehorn looked at the form:

CHECK REASON YOU HAVE TO SEE PRINCIPAL (that will save time)	
1 Talking in class	4 Unexcused absence
2 Chewing gum in class	5 Unexcused illness
3 Talking back to teacher	6 Unexcused behaviour
P.T.O.	

There were many things to check, but Treehorn couldn't find one that said 'Being Too Small to Reach the Water Bubbler'. He finally wrote in 'SHRINKING'.

When the lady said he could see the Principal, Treehorn went into the Principal's office with his form.

The Principal looked at the form, and then he looked at Treehorn. Then he looked at the form again.

'I can't read this,' said the Principal. 'It looks like SHIRKING. You're not SHIRKING, Treehorn? We can't have any shirkers here.

We're a team, and we all have to do our very best.'

'It says SHRINKING,' said Treehorn. 'I'm shrinking.'

'Shrinking, eh?' said the Principal. 'Well, now, I'm very sorry to hear that, Treehorn. You were right to come to me. That's what I'm here for. To guide. Not to punish, but to guide. To guide all the members of my team. To solve all their problems.'

'But I don't have any problems,' said Treehorn. 'I'm just shrinking.'

'Well, I want you to know I'm right here when you need me, Treehorn,' said the Principal, 'and I'm glad I was here to help you. A team is only as good as its coach, eh?'

The Principal stood up. 'Goodbye, Treehorn. If you have any more problems, come straight to me, and I'll help you again. A problem isn't a problem once it's solved, right?'

Florence Parry Heide, *The Shrinking of Treehorn*

Puzzles

Word study

These words all occur in this unit. The number after each one tells you the page it is on.

accommodation 5	nauseating 8
facilities 5	repulsive 8
hypnotized 7	aroma 9
fantasy 7	coincidence 10

1 Find each word and read the sentence it is in.
2 Write each word on a new line.
3 Against each one write what you think it means. If you do not know, have a guess.
4 Look *all* the words up in the dictionary.
5 Write the correct meanings of any that you got wrong.

Anagrams

These are all names that occur in this unit. The letters have been jumbled to make other names. Work out what they should be.

Watson's Brat	Patti Robetrex
Jon Pasto	Wallis Snit
Cal Snoreheim	Rene Roth

Gulliver arrives in Lilliput

This story has been divided into six sections. They have been printed in the wrong order. Write down the numbers in the correct order.

1   I was lying on my back and found my arms and legs were strongly fastened on each side to the ground. My hair, which was long and thick, was tied down in the same manner. I could only look upwards, the sun began to grow hot and the light hurt my eyes.

2   We set sail from Bristol, on May 4th 1699. At first all went well. But then a violent storm drove us off course. On the fifth of November the seamen spied a rock not far from the ship but the wind was so strong that we were driven onto it, and immediately split. Six of us let down the boat into the sea and tried to get clear of the ship and the rock.

3   I often let my legs drop and could feel no bottom. When I was almost gone and could struggle no longer, I found myself within my depth. At last I got to the shore.
     It was about eight o'clock in the evening. I walked nearly half a mile but could not discover any sign of houses or inhabitants. I was extremely tired.

4   I heard a confused noise about me, but from where I lay, I could see nothing except the sky.
     In a little time I felt something alive moving on my left leg. It moved gently forward over my breast and came almost up to my chin. I looked down as much as I could and saw that it was a man no more than six inches high, with a bow and arrow in his hands.

5   I lay down on the grass, which was very short and soft, and I slept sounder than I can ever remember.
     When I awaked it was just daylight. I attempted to rise but was not able to stir.

6   We rowed about three leagues, till we could work no longer. Shortly afterwards the boat was overturned.
     I cannot tell what happened to my companions, but I believe they were all lost. For my own part, I started to swim and was pushed along by wind and tide.

What games are being played here?
Have you played any of these games?
What are the rules?
What games did you play at your last school?

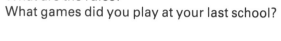

Hard Cheese

The grown ups are all safe,
Tucked up inside,
Where they belong.

They doze into the telly,
Bustle through the washing-up,
Snore into the fire,
Rustle through the paper.

They're all there,
Out of harm's way.

Now it's *our* street:
All the back yards,
All the gardens,
All the shadows,
All the dark corners,
All the privet hedges,
All the lamp-posts,
All the doorways.

Here is an important announcement:
The army of occupation
Is confined to barracks.
Hooray.

17

We're the natives.
We creep out at night,
Play everywhere,
Swing on *all* the lamp-posts,
Slit your gizzard?

Then, about nine o'clock,
They send out search parties.

We can hear them coming.
And we crouch
In the garden-sheds,
Behind the dustbins,
Up the alleyways,
Inside the dustbins,
Or stand stock-still,
And pull ourselves in,
As thin as a pin,
Behind the lamp-posts.

And they stand still,
And peer into the dark.
They take a deep breath –
You can hear it for miles –
And then, they bawl,

They shout, they caterwaul:
'J-i-i-i-i-mmeeee!'
'Timeforbed. D'youhearme?'
'M-a-a-a-a-reeee!'
'J-o-o-o-o-hnneeee!'
'S-a-a-a-a-mmeeee!'
'Mary!' 'Jimmy!'
'Johnny!' 'Sammy!'
Like cats. With very large mouths.

Then we give ourselves up,
Prisoners – of – war.
Till tomorrow night.

But just you wait.
One of these nights
We'll hold out,
We'll lie doggo,
And wait, and wait,
Till they just give up
And mumble
And go to bed.
You just wait.
They'll see!

Justin St. John

Questions to think and talk about

1 What does the writer think of grown-ups?
2 Do you agree with him?
3 Do you think that the street is your private place in the evenings?
4 Do you have some other special place that you think of as *yours*?
5 Do your parents have any places that they say are only theirs?
6 Should they have?
7 Are there enough playspaces in the area where you live?

Writing

1 Write a poem or description about your own street, or the place where you live. Choose one aspect to write about. For example: the children who live there; the street at different times or seasons; the people and the houses they live in.
2 Write a parents' version of *Hard Cheese*.
3 Write the story of what happens on the evening when the children 'lie doggo and wait and wait until they just give up'.

Tag

Tig, tag, tip, tap, dub, dab, tock, touch, he: what do you call it? Some people just call it 'it'. Whatever name you use, it is a game that everyone has played. One person chases the others and tries to capture them simply by touching them.

Everyone has played it, but not many know how it started. Why should just a touch be so frightening? It all goes back hundreds of years. Long ago people believed in spirits. These were creatures that you could not usually see unless they wanted you to. They lived in the fields and woods, in trees and in people's houses. Some were good and helped you. Others were evil and wanted to do harm. Some had names that we still recognize: goblins, trolls, gnomes, bogeys. Just a touch from an evil spirit worked like the most powerful poison. The only thing to do was run away.

So the game of touch, or tag, is a memory of running away from evil spirits. Most versions of the game, however, are more than just running away and being caught. Very often the person who is caught has to do something. He may have to freeze, as in the game called Chinese Lamp-posts, which reminds us that the spirits had the power to turn a man to stone. Or he might have to join up with the chaser, as in Chain Tag, because the spirits were able to force a man to do what they wanted.

There were, fortunately, things you could do to save yourself. In some places, iron was believed to be magic and if you touched it, you were safe. This led to Iron Tag. Wood, too, was good magic, so if you hung from the branch of a tree by your arms you would be safe – hence Off Ground Tag. Then there were special actions and words you could use to save yourself. You could make the sign of the cross, by crossing your fingers. Or you could say a magic word like 'Kings' or 'Crees' or 'Fains'. In games of tag such words are still used. We call them 'truce words'.

Today all that is left is a game that everyone knows. It has dozens of different versions. All you have to do, if you want a game of tag is shout out,

'Can't catch me –
Can't catch a flea . . .'

and start running!

Questions

1 How many different names are there for the game that is described here?
2 How long ago did it start?
3 Where did the spirits live?
4 Could people see them?
5 Were they all the same?
6 What happened if an evil spirit touched you?
7 What is the name of the game where you have to stay still when you are touched?
8 What do you do in Chain Tag?
9 How did Off Ground Tag start?
10 What are truce words?

What are the rules?

Writing   Write an explanation of the rules of this game so that someone who did not know how to play would be able to.
or
Choose another game of tag that you know and write the rules of that.

Hide and Seek

Call out. Call loud: 'I'm ready! Come and find me!'
The sacks in the toolshed smell like the seaside.
They'll never find you in this salty dark,
But be careful that your feet aren't sticking out.
Wiser not to risk another shout.
The floor is cold. They'll probably be searching
The bushes near the swing. Whatever happens
You mustn't sneeze when they come prowling in.
And here they are, whispering at the door;
You've never heard them sound so hushed before.
Don't breathe. Don't move. Stay dumb. Hide in your blindness.
They're moving closer, someone stumbles, mutters;
Their words and laughter scuffle, and they're gone.
But don't come out just yet; they'll try the lane
And then the greenhouse and back here again.
They must be thinking that you're very clever,
Getting more puzzled as they search all over.
It seems a long time since they went away.
Your legs are stiff, the cold bites through your coat;
The dark damp smell of sand moves in your throat.
Push off the sacks. Uncurl and stretch. That's better!
Out of the shed and call to them: 'I've won!
Here I am! Come and own up I've caught you!'
The darkening garden watches. Nothing stirs.
The bushes hold their breath; the sun is gone.
Yes, here you are. But where are they who sought you?

Vernon Scannell

The Goalkeeper's Revenge

Sim Dalt had two long, loose arms, spindly legs, a bony face with gleaming brown eyes, and, from the age of twelve, was reckoned to be a bit touched in the head.

Goalkeeping was the main interest in Sim's life. In his nursery days the one indoor pastime that satisfied him was when his mother kicked a rubber ball from the living-room into the kitchen, while Sim stood goal at the middle door. It was rare even then that he let one pass.

He later attended Scuttle Street elementary school, where he was always gnawed with the ferocious wish for four o'clock, when he could dash to the cinder park to play goalie for some team or other. Even in the hot summer days, Sim would cajole a few non-players into a game of football. 'Shoot 'em in, chaps,' he would yell, after lovingly arranging the heaps of jackets for the goal-posts, 'the harder the better.'

At twelve he was picked as goalkeeper for his school team. 'If you let any easy 'uns through,' the captain, Bob Thropper, threatened him, 'I'll bust your shins in!'

But he had no need to warn Sim, for it was rare indeed that anyone could get a ball past him.

It was near the end of the season, and Scuttle Street were at the top of the league and in the final for the Mayor's Shield, when a new and very thorough inspector visited the school. He found Sim's scholastic ability to be of such a low order that he directed him at once to Clinic Street special school.

'I suppose you could continue to play for us until the end of the season,' said Mr Speckle, at a meeting of the team, 'and then, at least, you'll be sure of a medal.'

'What, sir!' interposed Bob Thropper. 'A *cracky school* lad play for us? Ee, sir, that *would* be out of order!'

'But what shall we do about a goalkeeper?' asked the teacher.

'Goalkeepers!' snorted Bob, 'I could buy 'em and sell 'em.'

'What,' asked Sim, staring at Bob, 'what do you mean, "buy 'em an' sell 'em"?'

'I mean that they're ten a penny,' grunted Bob, 'especially daft 'uns.' And having made his point he snapped: 'Off with them togs, mate – we want 'em for our next man.' And Sim removed his boots, stockings, and shorts, but when it came to the jersey, he hesitated, but Bob grabbed at it: 'Buy 'em an' sell 'em,' he growled, 'that's me.'

There was a tear close to Sim's eye. 'I'll never buy you,' he hissed, 'but I might *sell* you one day.'

In adapting himself to his new life he was quick enough to grasp any advantage it might offer. He organized games in the schoolyard, and for two years enjoyed some hectic if not polished goalkeeping. And at the age of fifteen, when his mother took him round to different factories for work, he simulated idiocy so as not to be taken on.

'Now stop this shinanikin,' his mother scolded him, 'you're no more barmy than I am. And you know it.'

'You shoulda told the school-inspector that,' remarked Sim.

Every morning, with the 'normal intelligence' boys gaping enviously at him through the factory windows, Sim would set out for the cinder park bouncing and heading a football along the street.

At the age of nineteen he accepted his first job, since it did not interfere with his way of life; also, it had possibilities. It was at Brunt's Amusement Arcade, where the chief attraction was a 'Beat the Goalie' game. There were goal-posts that appeared to be full size, and a real football, and all comers were invited to try to score. It cost threepence for a try, and anyone who scored received sixpence in return. Sim, of course, got the job of goalkeeper.

Maggie Brunt, the owner, was a wizened, red-eyed woman. 'How's it goin', lad?' she would say, giving sly slaps of apparent goodwill on various parts of the goalkeeper's person. By this cunning form of greeting she had caught out a stream of employees who had been fiddling – having one pocket for Maggie and one for themselves.

She tried it out on Sim, time after time, and never once was there the faintest jingle of metal, until finally she decided that the lad must be simple, if not honest. The fact was that Sim – who did things with singular efficiency when he had to – had constructed a special pocket, copiously insulated with cottonwool, and provided with various sections for different coins. Had Maggie turned him upside-down and shaken him like a pepper-pot she would not have heard the faintest jingle, so expertly was it contrived.

There came a day, after some six thrifty years, when Maggie decided to sell the Arcade – and Sim was able to buy it from her. 'Bless you, lad,' sighed Maggie, 'they say you're gone in the head, but I wish there were more like you.'

'It wouldn't do,' remarked Sim, and not without a touch of regret he removed the cottonwool from his pocket.

Bob Thropper's visit to the Arcade was the start of a remarkably prosperous boom for Sim. Bob was a thickset, dark-jowled footballer by this time, and the idol of the Hummerton crowd. His tremendous kicking power had broken many goal-nets,

winded or knocked senseless a number of goalkeepers, and on one occasion, it was said, had actually smashed a crossbar.

One night, just after a cup-tie victory, Bob and his team-mates, merry though not drunk, were passing the Arcade, when one suggested having some sport with Sim.

'Skipper,' whispered Stan Mead, 'you smash one in!'

Stan Mead dived into his pocket for threepence, when Sim called out: 'Like to make it pounds instead of pence?'

The challenge was taken up at once, and in a moment eleven pound notes were flung down, and Sim covered these with as many out of his pocket. Then Bob Thropper drew back, took his short, confident run, and let go one of his famous drives. Sim was up like a flash, and brought it down with stylish assurance.

Then with a casual air he threw the ball back. 'Are you covering the twenty-two quid?' he asked.

The money was covered in two minutes. 'What about waiting till somebody nips off for your football boots?' asked Stan Mead.

Bob shook his head. 'I could lick this loon,' he snorted, 'in my bare feet' – and with that he took a second shot. It was good – but not good enough. Sim leapt and caught it on his chest. Bob's face went darker than ever. 'Fetch my boots,' he hissed at Stan Mead, 'an' I'll smash him to bits.'

A huge crowd swayed the Arcade when Bob Thropper prepared to make the third attempt. The forty-four pounds had been covered, so that there was a pile of pound notes on an orange box, with a brick on top of them. After having his boots tied up, Bob Thropper removed his jacket, took off his collar and tie, and nodded to Stan Mead to place the ball. The crowd went silent as he took the short run, and then kicked.

The ball flashed forward – it went like lightning, a knee-high shot. *'Goal!'* yelled a voice from behind. But a long thin figure whizzed through the air. There was a thud, the figure dropped to the ground. Nobody could be sure what had happened – until Sim stood up. His face was white. But he had the ball clutched against his heart. Slowly he went towards the orange box and picked up the money. 'Closing time!' he whispered in a low, clear voice. The crowd set up a sudden cheer – volley after volley.

From that night on Sim Dalt became famous as 'The goalie Bob Thropper could never beat!' The Arcade flourished. Sim got offers from many teams, including one from Hummerton club itself.

'When I join your club,' he told them, 'it'll not be as a goalie.'

And it was not many years before Sim's words came true, for there came a chance for him to buy a considerable portion of club shares, and he was voted a director.

One September morning early in the season he was taken round and introduced to all the players.

'Meet Bob Thropper,' said the co-director, 'our most famous centre-forward.'

Sim looked at the man before him. 'Centre-forwards,' he remarked significantly, 'I can buy 'em an' sell 'em – or,' he added, 'I can at least sell 'em.'

Some vague and long-forgotten moment of memory was evoked in Bob Thropper at these words.

He stood there frowning. Then, as Stan Mead nudged him and spoke, it all came back to him clearly.

'Bob, you'd better be looking for a nice pub to retire to,' Stan whispered feelingly, 'because this chap means it.'

Bill Naughton, *The Goalkeeper's Revenge*

The hyena and the villagers

This game comes from north Africa. Each player has to travel across the desert to the well and then back to the village. On the way back the villagers may be attacked and eaten by a fierce hyena.

Starting
Any number of people can play. You need the following: one dice; a board marked out like this:

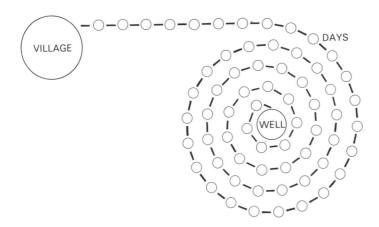

You can draw the diagram bigger on a large sheet of paper. The exact number of 'days' is not important.

You also need a different coloured counter for each player and one for the hyena.

The journey out

1 Players throw the dice to see who gets the highest score. This person starts.
2 Players must throw a six to start. This gets them to the first circle. More than one player can be on the same circle.
3 After that players move according to the dice as usual. A six gives a player another throw.
4 Players must throw the correct number to reach the well. If they do not, they must wait until they do.

The journey back

5 When the villagers reach the well they must stay there, getting water until they throw a six. This takes them onto the first space on their return journey.
6 It is not necessary to throw the exact number to get back into the village.

The hyena

7 The first player back becomes the hyena. He must throw a six to start. Then he moves *twice* the number shown on the dice.
8 When he reaches the well (exact number not needed) he turns round.
9 On the way back he 'eats' any villagers on whose circle he lands.

Winning
The winner is the person who becomes the hyena. Any villagers who get back to the village safely are runners-up.

Dwile flonking

According to the 'Waveney' rules of 1585 a team, traditionally dressed in smocks, straw hats, and straws in the mouth, forms a 'girter' or circle. The referee says, 'Here y'is t'gether,' and a man in the centre of the circle, the 'flonker', shouts 'dwiles away'. The flonker has a pole, or driveller, on top of which is perched an ullage-soaked dishcloth, and his task is to throw it at the dancing circle around him. A hit to the head is a 'wonton' and scores 3 points; a body hit, a 'morther', is worth 2 points and one to the leg, a 'ripper', is 1. The flonker is allowed two shots and if he doesn't score he is 'swadged' and 'potted', which means that he has to drink a 'potty' (six pints) of beer, while the circle chants 'pot, pot' and passes the dwile from hand to hand. If he fails to drain the pot in the time that it takes the dwile to go round the circle, he loses a point.

Arthur R. Taylor, *Pub Games*

What do you think is going on in this photograph?

Puzzles

Playing with words

Do you know the answers to these riddles?

1. How deep is the ocean?
2. How many balls of string would it take to reach the moon?
3. What goes up when the rain comes down?
4. What holds water yet is full of holes?
5. What did the bull say when it swallowed a bomb?
6. What did the big tap say to the little tap?
7. What can go up a chimney down but can't come down a chimney up?
8. Why did the hen run?
9. What did the monkey say as it cut off its tail?
10. What do you call an Arabian milk farmer?
11. What is the best thing to give as a parting gift?
12. How should you dress on a cold day?
13. What race is never run?
14. What ring is square?
15. Which driver never commits a traffic offence?
16. What sort of robbery is the easiest?
17. What is worse than raining cats and dogs?
18. What is the difference between a burglar and a man wearing a wig?
19. What bird is always out of breath?
20. Who gets the sack every time he goes to work?

Word square

The names of ten games are hidden in this square.
How many can you find?

```
M R A L T X S N A P P I
N O T U P L L Y I G N A
A C F D W N E G A I H M
E F O O F T A L B O O L
I A B S O N X E C T C I
I G N N E T B A L L K T
C H N G I E B O T O E D
D R T N O N O A Y U Y A
G R I E E N Y M L R F I
E D N C E I W G L L X I
S P U P K S N O O K E R
S O C T A E H T O L Y U
M Y A E W L T L B R F E
```

Jumbled story

This story has been divided into eight sections. They have been printed in the wrong order. Write down the numbers in the correct order.

1 His father was in the garden and looked up. Davie shouted again, 'Help! The room is on fire!'

2 She rushed out into the garden in alarm. Davie's brother was playing happily on the grass. Davie laughed and laughed.

3 He was playing with matches in his bedroom – which he knew was wrong. Accidentally he caught the bed on fire. He tried to put it out, but he couldn't.

4 Davie ended up in hospital. Now he thinks twice before playing practical jokes.

5 Davie was a great joker. He loved to fool people: parents, friends – everybody. One day he told his mother that his baby brother had fallen out of the window.

6 His father just smiled. 'Oh no,' he said, 'you don't catch me that way.'

7 'Fooled you!' he shouted. Davie was full of tricks like that, but one day he was caught out.

8 Soon the whole room was on fire and Davie was trapped. Davie rushed to the window and shouted for help.

Word study

These words all occur in this unit. The number after each one tells you the page it is on.

caterwaul	17	truce	18
sought	20	ferocious	21
wizened	22	apparent	22
prosperous	22	vague	24

1 Find each word and read the sentence it is in.
2 Write each word on a new line.
3 Against each one write what you think it means. If you do not know, have a guess.
4 Look *all* the words up in the dictionary.
5 Write the correct meanings of any that you got wrong.

TOOTH and CLAW

What are these animals?
Which of them live by eating other animals?
Is this cruel?

1

2

3

4

5

Trapped!

He turned and dashed back through the nearest gap in the hedge. On the instant, a fearful commotion began on the farther side. There were sounds of kicking and plunging. A stick flew into the air. Then a flat, wet clot of dead leaves shot clean through the gap and landed clear of the hedge, close to Hazel. The brambles thrashed up and down. Hazel and Fiver stared at each other, both fighting against the impulse to run. What enemy was at work on the other side of the hedge? There were no cries – no spitting of a cat, no squealing of a rabbit – only the crackling of twigs and the tearing of the grass.

By an effort of courage against all instinct, Hazel forced himself forward into the gap, with Fiver following. A terrible sight lay before them. The rotten leaves had been thrown up in showers. The earth had been laid bare and was scored with long scratches and furrows. Bigwig was lying on his side, his back legs kicking and struggling. A length of twisted copper wire, gleaming dully in the first sunlight, was looped round his neck and ran taut across one fore-paw to the head of a stout peg driven into the ground. The running knot had pulled tight and was buried in the fur behind his ear. The projecting point of one strand had lacerated his neck and drops of blood, dark and red as yew berries, welled one by one down his shoulder. For a few moments he lay panting, his side heaving in exhaustion. Then again began the struggling and fighting, backwards and forwards, jerking and falling, until he choked and lay quiet.

Frenzied with distress, Hazel leapt out of the gap and squatted beside him. Bigwig's eyes were closed and his lips pulled back in a fixed snarl. He had bitten his lower lip and from this, too, the blood was running. Froth covered his jaws and chest.

'Thlayli!' said Hazel, stamping. 'Thlayli! Listen! You're in a snare – a snare! Come on – think. How can we help you?'

There was a pause. Then Bigwig's back legs began to kick once more, but feebly. His ears drooped. His eyes opened unseeing and the whites showed blood-shot as the brown irises rolled one way and the other. After a moment his voice came thick and low, bubbling out of the bloody spume in his mouth.

'No good – biting wire. Peg – got to – dig out.'

A convulsion shook him and he scrabbled at the ground, covering himself in wet earth and blood. Then he was still again.

'Run, Fiver, run to the warren,' cried Hazel. 'Get the others – Blackberry, Silver. Be quick! He'll die.'

Richard Adams, *Watership Down*

Questions to think and talk about

1 What happens to Bigwig when he dashes through the hedge?
2 What do Hazel and Fiver want to do when they hear the noise on the other side of the hedge?
3 What do they see when they go through the gap?
4 What does Bigwig tell them to do?
5 Do you think there is any chance of saving Bigwig?

Writing

You are walking through a forest with a friend. Suddenly your friend falls into a deep hole in the ground which has been dug to trap an animal. There are sharp sticks in the hole which have hurt your friend. Write a story about what happens next.

The Indian tiger

The tiger is the most handsome and lordly of the big cats. While lions are top predators of the open country, tigers thrive where there is more cover. This is because the striped, black-brown markings of the tiger's coat make it difficult to spot amongst trees and bushes.

5   There are tigers in the snows of Siberia and in the steamy tropical rain forests of the East Indies. There are seven different types of tiger. Each type is particularly adapted to the type of country in which it is found.

    Tigers kill many different kinds of prey. They have been
10 known to kill animals as large as wild bull buffaloes, will take many species of deer and antelope, as well as wild pig, monkeys and porcupines, but also may eat very small prey like locusts. Tigers are excellent swimmers and can capture fish and turtles in marshy country.

15   The tiger will stalk very close to its prey using a powerful sense of smell and hearing rather than sight. Once within attacking distance, it will rush at its prey over a short distance. Usually it grasps at a shoulder with one clawed foot, then seizes the prey's throat from the underside. This action will break the neck of small
20 prey. Larger ones probably die from suffocation as the windpipe is crushed.

    Hungry or diseased tigers kill cattle and the most notorious of them become man-eaters. Man in turn will hunt the tiger. As a result, the tiger is now high on the list of animals which might
25 become extinct.

Adapted from **Philip Whitfield,** *The Hunters*

Questions

1 Name two places where tigers can be found.
2 How many different types of tiger are there?
3 Name three animals which the tiger will eat.
4 Can tigers swim?
5 How well can tigers hear and smell?
6 How close does a tiger come to its prey before attacking?
7 How do the animals which are attacked by a tiger die?
8 Describe how a tiger actually attacks its prey.
9 Why do some tigers attack cattle and men?
10 What might happen to the tiger in the next few years?

Like a domestic cat stalking a bird, the tiger uses every trick of positioning its sinuous body to get close to its prey. By creeping straight towards the prey animal and crouching close to the ground, the tiger reduces the area displayed to it.

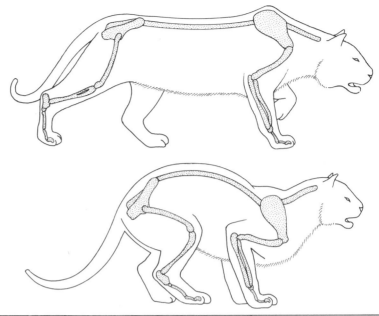

The final move in the tiger's attack on prey can be in the form of a rush or a leap depending on the type of terrain. This powerfully-muscled animal is on record as having made a single leap of 18 ft (5.6 m) from the ground to pull a man from a tree.

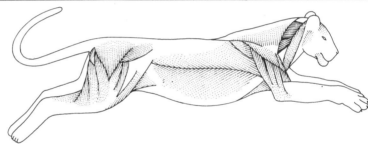

The prominent dark stripes on the tiger's coat must be the most familiar example of disruptive camouflage. Their function is to draw the prey animal's eye away from the tiger's body shape, which it would normally recognize and react to. The stripes enable the tiger to conceal itself in small clumps of vegetation and blend into the background.

The stripes never coincide with the real outline of the tiger's body but always run at right angles to it. An artificial tiger with stripes running with its outline would be hopelessly obvious and unable to camouflage itself successfully.

The Weasel

It should have been a moment
Of high drama,
The lithe, cigar-slim body,
The slight withdrawal and swift spring,
5   The soft explosion of black feathers . . .
But when I glided to a halt
And leaned from the car window
The blackbird had lost the duel
Of dignity,
10   And was being dragged,
Claws drooping palely
Upthrust on straw legs,
By the tiny killer,
Rump high, teeth gum-deep in feathers
15   Just above the two
Baby finger-nail eyelids.

The click of the ignition key
Startled the weasel
And through the verge grass he disappeared,
20   While the incongruous corpse
Stiffened in the dust.
But patience.
This plump prize whose blood
Is still, but still warm,
25   Is being watched,
And three anxious minutes pass
Before the grass
Parts,
The triangular, fawn head appears,
30   Looks up and down the lane,
Ignores the car,
And leaps to the carcass,
Drags it up the small cliff of the bank
And slides through the hedge backwards –
35   The whole action so neat,
Cool and efficient,
The work of a professional.

Gregory Harrison, *Posting Letters*

Killers

Can you say how these animals kill their prey?

Mountain Lion

Climbing through the January snow, into the Lobo Canyon
Dark grow the spruce-trees, blue is the balsam, water sounds
      still unfrozen, and the trail is still evident.

Men!
Two men!
Men! The only animal in the world to fear!

They hesitate.
We hesitate.
They have a gun.
We have no gun.

Then we all advance, to meet.

Two Mexicans, strangers, emerging out of the dark and snow and
      inwardness of the Lobo valley.
What are they doing here on this vanishing trail?

What is he carrying?
Something yellow.
A deer?

Qué tiene, amigo?
León –

He smiles, foolishly, as if he were caught doing wrong.
And we smile, foolishly, as if we didn't know.
He is quite gentle and dark-faced.

It is a mountain lion,
A long, long slim cat, yellow like a lioness.
Dead.

He trapped her this morning, he says, smiling foolishly.

Lift up her face,
Her round, bright face, bright as frost.
Her round, fine-fashioned head, with two dead ears;

And stripes in the brilliant frost of her face, sharp, fine dark rays,
Dark, keen, fine rays in the brilliant frost of her face.
Beautiful dead eyes.

Hermoso es!

They go out towards the open;
We go on into the gloom of Lobo.

And above the trees I found her lair,
A hole in the blood-orange brilliant rocks that stick up, a little cave.
And bones, and twigs, and a perilous ascent.

So, she will never leap up that way again, with the yellow flash of a
    mountain lion's long shoot!
And her bright striped frost-face will never watch any more, out of
    the shadow of the cave in the blood-orange rock,
Above the trees of the Lobo dark valley-mouth!

Instead, I look out.
And out to the dim of the desert, like a dream, never real;
To the snow of the Sangre de Cristo mountains, the ice of the
    mountains of Picoris,
And near across at the opposite steep of snow, green trees
    motionless standing in snow, like a Christmas toy.

And I think in this empty world there was room for me and a
    mountain lion.
And I think in the world beyond, how easily we might spare a
    million or two of humans
And never miss them.
Yet what a gap in the world, the missing white frost-face of that
    slim yellow mountain lion!

D. H. Lawrence

The wolves

He came out of a doze that was half nightmare, to see the she-wolf before him. She was not more than half a dozen feet away, sitting in the snow. The two dogs were whimpering and snarling at his feet, but she took no notice of them. She was looking at the man, and for some time he returned her look. There was nothing threatening about her. She looked at him merely with a great wistfulness, but he knew it to be the wistfulness of an equally great hunger. Her mouth opened, the saliva drooled forth, and she licked her chops with the pleasure of anticipation . . .

A spasm of fear went through him. He reached hastily for a brand to throw at her. But even as he reached, and before his fingers had closed on the missile, she sprang back into safety; and he knew that she was used to having things thrown at her.

All night, with burning brands, he fought off the hungry pack. When he dozed despite himself, the whimpering and snarling of the dogs aroused him. Morning came, but for the first time the light of day failed to scatter the wolves. The man waited in vain for them to go.

He made one desperate attempt to pull out on the trail. But the moment he left the protection of the fire, the boldest wolf leaped for him, but leaped short. He saved himself by springing back, the jaws snapping together a scant six inches from his thigh. The rest of the pack was now up and surging upon him, and a throwing of firebrands right and left was necessary to drive them back.

Even in the daylight he did not dare leave the fire to chop fresh wood. Twenty feet away towered a huge dead spruce. He spent half the day extending his campfire to the tree, at any moment a half dozen burning fagots ready at hand to fling at his enemies. Once at the tree, he studied the surrounding forest in order to fell the tree in the direction of the most firewood.

The night was a repetition of the night before, save that the need for sleep was becoming overpowering. The snarling of his dogs was losing its efficacy. Besides, they were snarling all the time, and his benumbed and drowsy senses no longer took note of changing pitch and intensity. He awoke with a start. The she-wolf was less than a yard from him. Mechanically, at short range, without letting go of it, he thrust a brand full into her open and snarling mouth. She sprang away, yelling with pain, and while he took delight in the smell of burning flesh and hair, he watched her shaking her head and growling wrathfully a score of feet away.

But this time, before he dozed again, he tied a burning pine-knot to his right hand. His eyes were closed but a few minutes when the burn of the flame on his flesh awakened him. For several hours he adhered to this program. Every time he was thus awakened he drove back the wolves with flying brands, replenished the fire, and rearranged the pine-knot on his hand. All worked well, but there came a time when he fastened the pine-knot insecurely. As his eyes closed it fell away from his hand.

He dreamed. It seemed to him that he was in Fort McGurry. It was warm and comfortable, and he was playing cribbage with the Factor. Also, it seemed to him that the fort was besieged by wolves. They were howling at the very gates, and sometimes he and the Factor paused from the game to listen and laugh at the futile efforts of the wolves to get in. And then, so strange was the dream, there was a crash. The door was burst open. He could see the wolves flooding into the big living-room of the fort. They were leaping straight for him and the Factor. With the bursting open of the door, the noise of their howling had increased tremendously. This howling now bothered him. His dream was merging into something else – he knew not what; but through it all, following him, persisted the howling.

And then he awoke to find the howling real. There was a great snarling and yelping. The wolves were rushing him. They were all about him and upon him. The teeth of one had closed upon his arm. Instinctively he leaped into the fire, and as he leaped, he felt the sharp slash of teeth that tore through the flesh of his leg. Then began a fire fight. His stout mittens temporarily protected his hands, and he scooped live coals into the air in all directions, until the camp-fire took on the semblance of a volcano.

But it could not last long. His face was blistering in the heat, his eyebrows and lashes were singed off, and the heat was becoming unbearable to his feet. With a flaming brand in each hand, he sprang to the edge of the fire. The wolves had been driven back. On every side, wherever the live coals had fallen, the snow was sizzling, and every little while a retiring wolf, with wild leap and snort and snarl, announced that one such live coal had been stepped upon.

Flinging his brands at the nearest of his enemies, the man thrust his smouldering mittens into the snow and stamped about to cool his feet. His two dogs were missing, and he well knew that they had served as a course in the protracted meal which had begun days before with Fatty, the last course of which would likely be himself in the days to follow.

'You ain't got me yet!' he cried, savagely shaking his fist at the hungry beasts.

He set to work to carry out a new idea that had come to him. He extended the fire into a large circle. Inside this circle he crouched, his sleeping outfit under him as a protection against the melting snow. When he had thus disappeared within his shelter of flame, the whole pack came curiously to the rim of the fire to see what had become of him. Hitherto they had been denied access to the fire, and they now settled down in a close-drawn circle, like so many dogs, blinking and yawning and stretching their lean bodies in the unaccustomed warmth. Then the she-wolf sat down, pointed her nose at a star, and began to howl. One by one the wolves joined her, till the whole pack, on haunches, with noses pointed skyward, was howling its hunger cry.

Dawn came, and daylight. The fire was burning low. The fuel had run out, and there was need to get more. The man attempted to step out of his circle of flame, but the wolves surged to meet him. Burning brands made them spring aside, but they no longer sprang back. In vain he strove to drive them back. As he gave up and stumbled inside his circle, a wolf leaped for him, missed, and landed with all four feet in the coals. It cried out with terror, at the same time snarling, and scrambled back to cool its paws in the snow.

The man sat down on his blankets in a crouching position. His body leaned forward from the hips. His shoulders, relaxed and drooping, and his head on his knees advertised that he had given up the struggle. Now and again he raised his head to note the dying down of the fire. The circle of flame and coals was breaking into segments with openings in between. These openings grew in size, the segments diminished.

'I guess you can come an' get me any time,' he mumbled. 'Anyway, I'm goin' to sleep.'

Once he wakened, and in an opening in the circle, directly in front of him, he saw the she-wolf gazing at him.

Again he awakened a little later, though it seemed hours to him. A mysterious change had taken place – so mysterious a change that he was shocked wider awake. Something had happened. He could not understand at first. Then he discovered it. The wolves were gone. Remained only the trampled snow to show how closely they had pressed him. Sleep was gripping him again, his head was sinking down upon his knees, when he roused with a sudden start.

There were cries of men, the churn of sleds, the creaking of harnesses, and the eager whimpering of straining dogs. Four sleds pulled in from the river bed to the camp among the trees. Half a dozen men were about the man who crouched in the centre of the dying fire. They were shaking and prodding him into consciousness. He looked at them like a drunken man and maundered in strange, sleepy speech:

'Red she-wolf . . . Come in with the dogs at feedin' time . . . First she ate the dog-food . . . Then she ate the dogs . . . An' after that she ate Bill . . .'

Jack London, *White Fang*

On the kill

In this passage some words have been left out. Read the story and try to work out what the words should be. Then write down the number of each space and the word you think should go there.

If the hunt has been successful ....¹..... pride at once runs towards the ....²..... . Licking their lips, the cubs fall ....³..... the carcass. Cubs and lionesses lie ....⁴..... to shoulder, forming a tight-packed ....⁵..... around the kill. But before they ....⁶..... had time to settle down the ....⁷..... himself arrives. Without hesitating, he plunges ....⁸..... into the circle, pushing females and ....⁹..... aside.

If the kill is large, ...¹⁰...., females and cubs tuck in together. ....¹¹.... there is plenty of meat for ....¹².... there is little cause for jealousy, ...¹³.... this does not rule out squabbles ....¹⁴.... claims for particular delicacies. But if ....¹⁵.... kill is small and there is ....¹⁶.... enough meat to satisfy the entire ....¹⁷...., the male will simply grab ....¹⁸.... carcass and run off to enjoy ....¹⁹.... on his own.

From the ring ....²⁰.... blood-smeared faces buried in the ....²¹...., the sounds of eating are punctuated ....²².... a chorus of low growls and ....²³..... . Squabbles often break into short, sharp ....²⁴...., stopping as quickly as they begin. ....²⁵.... and claws are in constant use, ...²⁶.... as much in defending some morsel ....²⁷.... a litter mate as in tearing ....²⁸.... the carcass. The flash of teeth ....²⁹.... the swipe of paws are an ....³⁰.... part of the proceedings.

Each member ....³¹.... the pride stuffs itself until it ....³².... eat no more. By the time ....³³.... lion has eaten all he can ....³⁴.... moved away he is so full ....³⁵.... his tummy almost touches the ground. ....³⁶.... swings uncomfortably at every step. The ....³⁷.... finds it an effort to walk ....³⁸.... the shade of a nearby tree. ....³⁹.... he collapses on the ground to ....⁴⁰.... off the effects of overeating. He ....⁴¹.... panting with exhaustion, barely able to ....⁴².... the energy to flick his tail ....⁴³.... drive away the hordes of flies. ....⁴⁴.... the fresh meat has given him ....⁴⁵.... thirst. So before long, if water ....⁴⁶.... close, he stirs himself to move ....⁴⁷.... a nearby waterhole to drink before ....⁴⁸.... his rest. The cubs, too, are ....⁴⁹.... after their meal. While the lionesses ....⁵⁰.... on the ground the cubs clamber ....⁵¹.... them to suckle.

Noel Simon, *Lions*

Puzzles

Crossword

This crossword is all to do with survival in the animal world. Copy it out and see how many of the clues you can solve.

Across

1 This word is used to describe any animal which kills other animals.
6 Fish live in the . . . .?
7 *We* eat this fish with chips!
9 An animal which has completely disappeared from the earth is . . . .?
10 What do spiders spin to catch their prey?
13 Where you will find many of the most dangerous animals in the world.
15 All swimmers should avoid this fish.
16 This animal was our ancestor!
17 This is what all animals hope to do.

Down

1 The fiercest British freshwater fish is a . . . .?
2 This is what all animals want to do when they are in danger.
3 The only poisonous snake in the British Isles.
4 Beast of burden.
5 You put this in a trap or on a fishing line.
8 A small but very dangerous fish with razor-sharp teeth.
11 This is a fierce cousin of the farmyard pig.
12 These insects have a sting in their tails.
14 From its hiding place a tiger might . . . . at its prey.

In this unit you are a policeman or policewoman. You are called to the scene of a serious accident and have to find out what happened. Go through the unit page by page. On each page you will find out new information about the accident. As you do so, write a report in your notebook. At the end of the unit, you have to write up your final report.

Accident at Salter's Cliff

43

First aid

53

When I reached the scene, the ambulance had already arrived. Its crew were attending to a number of injured people...

Write your report of what you saw when you arrived.

45

The car-driver's story

Write your report of what the driver told you.

The schoolteacher's story

57

The minibus had been driven by a schoolteacher, Miss Jean Starmer. She seemed dazed and confused when I interviewed her...

Write your report of what she told you.

Clues

Write your report. Describe what you found and what you thought it meant.

59

I then examined the scene of the accident in more detail...

Just a few questions . . .

61

It seemed clear to me that Miss Starmer had been telling the truth when she said that a car had been parked just round the corner. I knew that there was a Lea Road in Saltmouth. I made a copy of the tyre pattern and then travelled to 74 Lea Road.

Write your report of what you discovered when you interviewed the man.

Official report

Now you have to write your official report of the accident. This is the document that will be used by senior police officers to decide if anyone should be prosecuted. If there is a trial it will be used by the lawyers. Therefore it should be written in a way that they will understand and contain the details they need to get a clear idea of what happened.

You should use the following headings:

REPORT OF ROAD TRAFFIC ACCIDENT

Exact location
Date and time of accident
Vehicles involved
Casualties
Plan of site
Evidence found on site
Interviews with witnesses
Conclusions

Instructions
1 Work out in rough what you are going to write for each of these headings.
2 Work out what the plan of the site should show. (There is a plan of the road, without any cars, on page 50.)
3 Check it all through to make sure that you haven't made any mistakes.
4 Write out the final report.

Plan of site

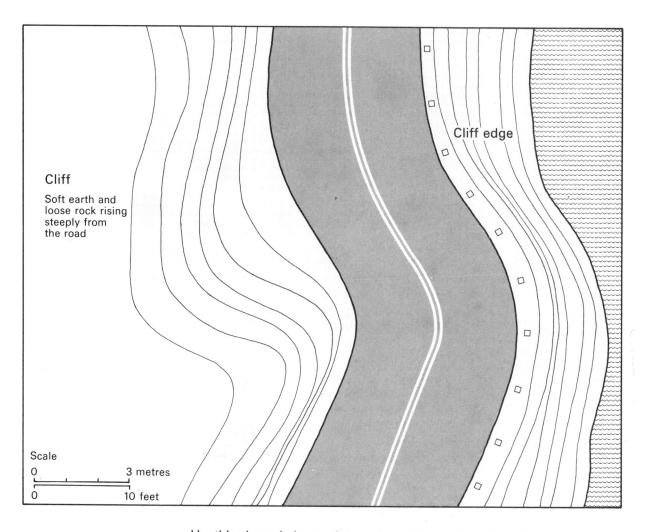

Cliff

Soft earth and
loose rock rising
steeply from
the road

Cliff edge

Scale

0   3 metres

0   10 feet

Use this plan to help you draw a plan of the accident. Copy it out and then
draw onto it the positions of the vehicles after the crash. Add any other
information that will help people to get a clear idea of what things looked like
when you arrived at the scene of the accident.

EMERGENCY

What would you do if you saw one of these incidents?

Flood

Albie slept more soundly than he'd slept since the family had been gone. He slept so soundly that he did not hear the first faint tapping raindrops, he did not hear the tapping increase to a steady fall. And he did not hear the heavy rumble that swelled to a roar as the wall of water that had breached and demolished the levee★ five miles to the north swept down the river, spread across fields, toppled trees, demolished bridges, swallowed animals, carried entire villages before and under its assault.

The house that had survived almost thirty years was lifted and rotated and tipped almost over and leveled and rotated again.

Albie was screaming as the water poured through doors and windows and cracked walls and up through the shattered flooring. He was still screaming when he at last fought free of the rug in which he'd wrapped himself.

He tried to stand, but the water tossed him back and forth, from wall to wall. His hands and knees, once, twice, scraped rough surfaces he tried to grasp. Then he was on the stairs leading up toward the bedrooms. The water, at whatever step he was holding to, swirled above his waist.

Coughing, gagging, Albie pulled himself up until, on the fourth step from the top, he was clear of the water. Though he knew he was at the top of the stairs, he felt as if he were descending. He waited. If the water was below him and he was escaping it, he had to be climbing *up*. While he waited, thinking, the house continued to shift and rotate, like a wood chip caught in a series of whirlpools.

He could see nothing in the darkness, but he could hear. He could hear the rain falling and he could hear the wind crackling and he could hear the water slapping the walls of the house.

★levee: embankment

At the top of the stairs, on the landing, he paused to rest. He coughed out more of the water, and he sat with his back against a wall for support. Shivering, clutching his arms around his chest, he tried to make sense out of what had happened. All he could do was shiver and cough.

Albie stood and staggered along the hallway. The first room on the left was his parents' bedroom. He found the door, but it would not open. Farther down the hall, on the opposite side, was his bedroom. The door, open, was hanging by the top hinge only. Inside the room, Albie went to the window. He could see nothing. It was as black outside as it was inside.

He picked his way about the room, stumbling over an upturned chair. He set it upright and pushed it to the window and sat in it, a blanket tight around his body.

He was still too dazed, too exhausted, to think clearly. He dozed, jerked awake, dozed again, awakened again, until he realized that he was staring, fully awake, at the pale gray light that filled the window.

Albie threw off his blanket and ran to examine the damage the water had delivered to the barn.

The barn was gone.

A vast endless plain of water lay outside, flowing, hovering, a foot or two below the windowsill, slapping and sloshing against the exterior walls of the house. From this window the barn was always in full view, but now it was gone – washed away. So was the milk house, so was the smokehouse, so was the toilet, so were the pig pens and the chicken coops. Everything . . . everything was gone. Where all the buildings had been there was only that flat viscous sheet of brown fluid.

The house shook, like a dog throwing off water; it tilted and rotated to the left and rotated back, to the right. A tall grove of poplars drifted by, screened by the rain and the gray morning light. They disappeared.

How could trees remain upright when they floated?

Chester Aaron, *An American Ghost*

Questions to think
and talk about

1 What were Albie's first feelings when he woke up?
2 Why was it all so confusing?
3 Why was he so surprised when he looked out of the window?
4 What do you think had happened to the house?

Writing

The next four sentences in the story explain what had happened to the house. Write down what you think those four sentences might be. Then continue the story of what happened to Albie.

Fire

Fire is NEVER funny, NEVER a lark, NEVER a good joke.
Fire is **always** SERIOUS, **always** DANGEROUS.
Fire can KILL by BURNING, KILL by SUFFOCATION, KILL by SHOCK, KILL by POISONING.

Which things burn? Here are just some things:

The bodies of **people** – children, men, women.
The **clothes** people wear – cotton, silk, rayon, wool mixtures, winceyette, etc.
Many **toys** children play with – wooden ones, some cuddly ones, some plastic ones.
Things houses are **built** with – wood, plaster, fibre board, etc.
Fuels houses are **heated** with – coal and coke, gas, oil, wood.
Things houses are **decorated** with – paint, varnish, some plastics, polystyrene, etc.
Things houses are **furnished** with – furniture: the wood and the stuffing, curtains, covers, cushions, wooden beds, mattresses, blankets, sheets, pillows.

How can things be made to burn?
By being lit with – matches and other lighters, electric sparks, the hot sun.

How do fires start?

1 By **children** setting light to things.
2 By fires being left **unguarded** or not guarded well enough.
3 By **curtains** blowing on to stoves or candles.
4 By **smokers** throwing matches and cigarettes down when they are not quite out.
5 When electricity, gas and oil are not **used** properly.
6 When things which burn very easily are not **stored** properly.
7 When chimneys are not swept regularly.
8 When glass is caught by the sun's rays (e.g. mirrors left on window sills), etc.

How do fires spread?

1 When the things around burn easily.
2 If there is a wind or draught.
3 By the air around getting very hot. This hot air (and the smoke) rises and sets things alight as it goes.
4 By hot metals conducting heat to things which burn.

Remember

It isn't only flames which kill people.

People die very quickly when they breathe in SMOKE – it chokes and
    poisons.

People die very quickly when they breathe in HOT AIR.

Angela Creese, *Safety For Your Family*

Questions
1 Apart from burning, how else can fire kill?
2 Which materials used for making clothes will burn?
3 Which materials used for building houses will burn?
4 Which parts of a bed will burn?
5 How can smokers cause fires?
6 How can the sun cause a fire?
7 How does smoke kill people?
8 How does hot air kill people?
9 Look at the picture below. Make a list of all the possible causes of
    fire you can see.

Research   Find out the answers to these questions.
1 Where is the nearest fire extinguisher to where you are sitting?
2 How is it operated?
3 What is the fire alarm?
4 What should you do when you hear it?
5 Suppose you hear the alarm and you are quite sure it is a false
    alarm, what should you do?

How fires happen

I was alone in the house when it happened. I had been rendering
down a great quantity of beef fat. When I had finished I placed the
basin of liquid fat on the kitchen floor and put a frying pan of water
on the electric hotplate, with the intention of cooking myself some
kippers. Then I went to answer the telephone. The conversation
lasted some ten minutes.

Exactly as I put the receiver down there was a muffled but
heavy explosion from the kitchen. Tearing through into the living
room I looked aghast at the entrance to the small kitchen. The whole
doorway was blotted out in a roaring mass of flames whose tongues
were even now shooting along the living-room rafters. Just inside
the main door of the house was a large new fire-extinguisher. I seized
this impressive weapon rapidly and carried out the simple instructions
printed upon it. I advanced as near to the flames as the heat allowed
me, and directed the nozzle towards the kitchen ceiling.

The jet of fluid lasted for something less than three seconds,
Then this aggressive and brightly coloured instrument just began to
dribble on the floor. The only tap in the house lay beyond the wall
of flames and the nearest water out of doors was Teko's★ pool. I
grabbed two buckets and raced for it. The bolt on his gate was
stuck: by the time I had the two buckets full and the gate closed
behind me I thought there was little chance of saving the house. It is
entirely lined with the ideal tinder of Oregon pine-panelling. The
first buckets had little effect beyond a blinding cloud of steam. Eight
times I ran to and fro between the pool and the kitchen, throwing
the water to the ceiling in cupped hands. After the last of these
nightmare journeys, I was amazed to see that no flame remained.
The kitchen walls and ceiling, which had been repainted a week
before, were charred and blackened, but no living spark was left.

The first thing to catch my eye among the dismal debris was the
remains of something that looked like the casing of a small home-
made bomb: the ragged strips of thin, twisted metal that result from
an explosion within a container. There was a considerable number
of these scattered round the room, and then quite suddenly I saw
their origin. Embedded in the basin of fat was the warhead – the
upper half of a deodorant spray of popular make. This tin,
evidently, had stood too close to the hotplate on which I had
prepared to cook my kippers. It had exploded, and with awful

★ Teko was a pet otter

40 accuracy had travelled eight feet to slam into the basin of liquid fat. The force of the impact had sprayed fat all over the walls and ceiling. Enough had fallen on the hotplate to start the fire, and this had in turn detonated two more deodorant cans, several pieces of which had also found their way into the fat and given fresh impetus to the flames.

adapted from **Gavin Maxwell,** *The Rocks Remain*

This fire might not have been so devastating if Gavin Maxwell had taken some precautions and had known the correct way to deal with a fire caused by burning fat. Great care should be taken with hot fat both during and after cooking to prevent it catching fire. If you have to deal with a pan of burning fat, the Royal Society for the Prevention of Accidents (ROSPA) recommends: 'Switch off the heat. Cover the pan with a lid or damp cloth. Don't move the pan or throw water on it.' *Kitchen Fire Safety*

Framed in a first-storey winder

Framed in a first-storey winder of a burnin' buildin'
Appeared: A Yuman 'Ead!
'Jump into this net wot we are 'oldin'
And yule be quite orl right!'

But 'e wouldn't jump . . .

And the flames grew Igher and Igher and Igher.
(Phew!)

Framed in a second-storey winder of a burnin' buildin'
Appeared: A Yuman 'Ead!
'Jump into this net wot we are 'oldin'
And yule be quite orl right!'

But 'e wouldn't jump . . .

And the flames grew Igher and Igher and Igher . . .
(Strewth!)

Framed in a third-storey winder of a burnin' buildin'
Appeared: A Yuman 'Ead!
'Jump into this net wot we are 'oldin'
And yule be quite orl right!
Honest!'

And 'e jumped . . .

And 'e broke 'is bloomin' neck!

Anon.

Tornado

It was raining lightly on May 14th 1962, and spring showers are always welcome in the Great Plains. Farmer Emil Ziebart of Ethan, a town in south-eastern South Dakota, glanced at the churning clouds massing in the south-west. He decided that there was just time to plough another furrow before supper. Nearing the end of the round, he checked the sky again. A greyish-black cloud wall about half a mile wide loomed over his neighbour's tree grove. Below it hung a funnel-shaped mass, tapering towards the earth. Then suddenly, as he stared, horrified, the trees disappeared, flicked up as easily as a vacuum cleaner sucks up dust specks.

He jerked the plough from the earth and turned the tractor towards home. Behind him, advancing, the cavernous cloud mouth gaped hungrily.

He jumped from the tractor, raced towards the shelter belt of trees on the west side of his farmyard, dived headfirst through the wire fence and grabbed the nearest treetrunk. There was a strange, ominous silence. Emil Ziebart gasped for breath in the weighted Stygian★ air. He could hear only the pounding of his heart. Then there was a stupendous Niagara of sound and he felt a heavy blow on his back. He dug his face into the ground as the tornado roared over him.

Soon the black, omnivorous wall, the pressure, the horrifying noise were gone. Ziebart raised his head slowly. The top of the tree he was clutching was not there. Uprooted trees lay grotesquely like piles of rotting weeds, their roots hanging limp. Twisted, spiky pieces of tin, shattered lumber, an overturned corn-picker, huge drifts of last year's corn stalks, dead chickens – all lay in chaotic heaps as far as he could see. Beside him was a naked pheasant, only its remaining neck plumage identifying the lifeless form.

Dazed, Ziebart stood up. He shook his head. Something was wrong. He must be confused about directions, he decided. Where were the barn, the granary, the chicken houses – all his buildings? Gone. There was nothing standing, just mountains of debris.

Fearfully, he peered beyond for his house. He saw the remains of the front steps, leading up into empty space. Then he saw his home, completely lifted from the foundations, jammed against the tortured trees, roof fragments dangling pitifully like shattered human limbs. And his family?

★ Stygian: dark and gloomy

He scrambled drunkenly over the littered mess. 'Oh God! They're dead! It's taken everything. They're gone!' It was the immemorial cry of man against nature's cruelty.

Emeline Ziebart had not turned on the radio or TV that May afternoon, and did not hear the tornado warnings. While her freshly-baked banana cake cooled on the kitchen table, she put several loaves of bread into the oven. She noticed it was raining outside. Suddenly, an explosive crash startled her. The house shuddered convulsively; windows popped out.

'Tornado!' she shouted. 'Joey! Diane! Run for the basement!'

The three dashed wildly into the basement and crouched beneath the stairs, seven-year-old Joey between his mother and his sister, Diane, 17. Instinctively Mrs Ziebart pushed Joey down flat, she and Diane protecting his body with theirs. Superhuman powers pressed them viciously against the cement floor.

Then – was it one minute later, or five? – everything was quiet. The tornado had passed over them, its suction taking even their hiding place, the stairs. Above them was the open sky. Wreckage surrounded them – the washing machine, tubs, heavy pipes, severed electric cables, lumber – and mud everywhere. As they clambered out of the basement into the yard, fears flashed through Emeline Ziebart's mind. Where was Emil? Crushed beneath the tractor? Dashed to pieces in the field?

Suddenly she saw her husband – and he saw them at the same moment. He began to run, stumbling over the rubble. The four met and silently clung to one another. It was Diane who spoke first: 'Thank God! We're all alive!'

Helen Rezatto

The emergency services

Fire
Police
Ambulance
Coastguard
(for coastal and
sea rescue)

It is worth remembering how to
dial 999 in darkness or smoke.

Call the Operator
by dialling 999

or as shown on your dial label or dialling instructions

Tell the operator the emergency service you want

Give your exchange and number or all-figure number as appropriate

Wait until the Emergency authority answers

Then give them the full address where help is needed and other necessary information

Place two fingers in the two holes
directly to the left of the finger stop.
Remove finger nearest stop.

With finger in '9' hole rotate dial to
finger stop. Remove finger and
allow dial to return. Repeat
operation twice more.

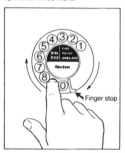

WAYNE: Hallo . . .

OPERATOR: Emergency. Which service do you want?

WAYNE: Is that Emergency? There's been a terrible accident and I
want you to do something about it. You see there was this little
girl and –

OPERATOR: Will you tell me which service you want, please.

WAYNE: and . . . and . . . somehow she got into this empty house.
And I was just –

OPERATOR: Which service, Fire, Police or Ambulance?

WAYNE: Oh, yes please. Anyway, there's been a fire and I –

OPERATOR: What number are you speaking from?

WAYNE: Number? Oh yes. Er, Clehonger 3567.

OPERATOR: Thank you. I'm putting you through.

FIRE STATION: Hullo. Fire Service. Will you tell me the exact site of
the fire, please.

WAYNE: Oh, yes. Well as I was just telling that nice lady at the
exchange, there's this little girl, you see and she got into this
empty house. I was just walking along the street, you see . . .

The Eighteenth Emergency

The pigeons flew out of the alley in one long swoop and settled on the awning of the grocery store. A dog ran out of the alley with a torn Cracker Jack box in his mouth. Then came the boy.

The boy was running hard and fast. He stopped at the sidewalk, looked both ways, saw that the street was deserted and kept going. The dog caught the boy's fear, and he started running with him.

Suddenly the boy slowed down, went up some stairs and entered an apartment building. The dog stopped. He sensed that the danger had passed, but he stood for a moment at the bottom of the stairs.

Inside the building the boy was still running. He went up the stairs three at a time, stumbled, pulled himself up by the banister and kept going until he was safely inside his own apartment. Then he sagged against the door.

His mother was sitting on the sofa, going over some papers. The boy waited for her to look up and ask him what had happened. He thought she should be able to hear something was wrong just from the terrible way he was breathing. 'Mom,' he said.

'Just a minute. I've got to get these orders straight.' When she went over her cosmetic orders she had a dedicated, scientific look. He waited until she came to the end of the sheet.

'Mom.' Without looking up, she turned to the next page. He said again, *'Mom.'*

'I'm almost through. There's a mistake some –'

He said, 'Never mind.' He walked heavily through the living room and into the hall. He threw himself down on the day bed.

His mother said, 'I'm almost through with this, Benjie.'

'I said, "Never mind."' He looked up at the ceiling. In a blur he saw a long cobweb hanging by the light fixture. A month ago he had climbed on a chair, written UNSAFE FOR PUBLIC SWINGING and drawn an arrow to the cobweb. It was still there.

He closed his eyes. He was breathing so hard his throat hurt.

'Benjie, come back,' his mother called. 'I'm through.'

'Never *mind.*'

'Come on, Benjie, I want to talk to you.'

He got up slowly and walked into the living room. She had put her order books on the coffee table. 'Sit down. Tell me what's wrong.' He hesitated and then sat beside her on the sofa. She waited and then said again, 'What's wrong?'

He did not answer for a moment. He looked out of the

window, and he could see the apartment across the street. A yellow cat was sitting in the window watching the pigeons. He said in a low voice, 'Some boys are going to kill me.'

'Not *kill* you, Benjie,' she said. 'No one is –'

He glanced quickly at her. 'Well, how do I know what they're going to do?' he said, suddenly angry.

'They're chasing me, that's all I know. When you see somebody chasing you, and when it's Marv Hammerman and Tony Lionni and a boy in a black sweat shirt you don't stop and say, "Now, what *exactly* are you guys planning to do – kill me or just break a few arms and legs?"'

'What did you do to these boys?'

'What did *I* do? I didn't do anything. You think I would do something to Marv Hammerman who is the biggest boy in my school? He should be in high school.'

'I know you did something. I can always tell. Now, what happened?'

'Nothing, Mom. I didn't do anything.' He looked down at his shoes. With his foot he began to kick at the rug. A little mound of red lint piled up in front of his tennis shoe.

'They wouldn't be after you for nothing.'

'Well, they are.' He paused. He knew he had to give an explanation, but he could not give the right one. He said, 'Maybe Hammerman just doesn't like me. I don't know. I'm not a mind reader.'

'Look at me, Benjie.'

Without looking up he said, 'Mom, just listen to what Hammerman did to this boy in my room one time. This boy was in line in the cafeteria and Hammerman came up to him and –'

'What I want to hear is what happened *today*, Benjie.'

'Just *listen*. And this boy in the cafeteria was standing in line, Mom, doing absolutely nothing, and Hammerman comes up to him and –'

'Benjie, what happened *today*?'

He hesitated. He looked down at his tennis shoe. There was a frayed hole in the toe, and he had taken a ballpoint pen and written AIR VENT and drawn a little arrow pointing to the hole.

'What happened?' she asked again.

'Nothing.' He did not look at her.

'Benjie –'

'Nothing happened.'

She sighed, then abruptly she looked up. 'The beans!' She walked to the kitchen, and he lay back on the sofa and closed his eyes.

'Benjie?' He looked up. His mother was leaning around the door, looking at him. 'Why don't you watch television? Get your mind off yourself. That always helps me.'

'No, it won't help.'

'Well, let's just see what's on.' She came back in, turned on the television and waited for the set to warm up. He closed his eyes. He knew there was nothing on television that could interest him.

'Tarzan!' his mother said. 'You always have loved Tarzan.'

He opened his eyes and glanced at the screen. In the depths of the jungle, a hunter had stumbled into quicksand, and Tarzan was swinging to the rescue.

'All the hunter has to do,' he said with a disgusted sigh, 'is lie down on the quicksand and not struggle and he won't sink.'

'That wouldn't leave anything for Tarzan to do though, would it?' his mother said, smiling a little.

'Oh, I don't know.' He closed his eyes and shifted on the sofa. After a minute he heard his mother go back into the kitchen. He opened his eyes. On the screen the hunter was still struggling. Cheetah was beginning to turn nervous somersaults. Tarzan was getting closer.

Once he and his friend Ezzie had made a list of all the ways they knew to stay alive. Ezzie had claimed he could stay alive in the jungle forever. Ezzie said every jungle emergency had a simple solution.

Lying on the sofa, he tried to remember some of those old emergencies.

A second one came into his mind. Emergency Two – Attack by an Unfriendly Lion. Lion attack, Ezzie claimed, was an everyday occurrence in the jungle. What you had to do to survive was wait until the last moment, until the lion was upon you, and then you had to ram your arm all the way down the lion's throat. This would choke him and make him helpless. It was bound to be a little unpleasant, Ezzie admitted, to be up to your shoulder in lion, but that couldn't be helped.

'Is the Tarzan movie any good?' his mother asked from the kitchen.

'No.' He reached out and turned off the television. He sighed. Nothing could take his mind off Marv Hammerman for long.

'If it makes you feel any better,' his mother said, 'Teddy Roosevelt had the same problem. I saw it on television. Boys used to pick on him and chase him.'

'No, it doesn't,' he said. He waited a minute and then asked, 'What did Teddy Roosevelt do about it?'

'Well, as I remember it, Teddy's father got him a gymnasium and Teddy exercised and got strong and nobody ever picked on him again.'

'Oh.'

'Of course, it wasn't the same as – '

'Don't bother getting me a gymnasium.'

'Now, Benjie, I didn't – '

'Unless you know of some exerciser that gives instant muscles.' He thought about it for a minute. He would go out, exerciser in his pocket, and say, 'Here I am, Hammerman.' Then, just when Hammerman was stepping toward him, he would whip out the exerciser, pump it once, and muscles would pop out all over his body like balloons.

'Well, you'll handle it,' his mother said. 'In a few weeks you'll look back on this and laugh.'

'Sure.'

He lay with his eyes closed, trying to remember some more of the old ways he and Ezzie knew to survive life's greatest emergencies.

Emergency Three – Unexpected Charge of an Enraged Bull. Bulls have a blind spot in the centre of their vision, so when being charged by a bull, you try to line yourself up with this blind spot.

'Fat people can't do it, Mouse,' Ezzie had told him. 'That's why you never see any fat bullfighters. You and I can. We just turn sideways like this, see, get in the blind spot and wait.'

He could remember exactly how Ezzie had looked, waiting sideways in the blind spot of the imaginary bull. 'And there's one other thing,' Ezzie had added. 'It will probably work for a rhinoceros too.'

Emergency Four – Crocodile Attack. When attacked by a crocodile, prop a stick in its mouth and the crocodile is helpless.

At one time this had been his own favourite emergency. He had spent a lot of time dreaming of tricking crocodiles. He had imagined himself a tornado in the water, handing out the sticks like party favours. 'Take that and that and that!' The stunned crocodiles, mouths propped open, had dragged themselves away. For the rest of their lives they had avoided children with sticks in their hands. 'Hey, no!' his dream crocodiles had cried, 'Let that kid alone. He's got sticks, man, *sticks*!'

Abruptly he turned his head toward the sofa. The smile which had come to his face when he had remembered the crocodiles now faded. He pulled a thread in the slip cover. The material began to pucker, and he stopped pulling and smoothed it out. Then he took a pencil from his pocket and wrote in tiny letters on the wall PULL THREAD IN CASE OF BOREDOM and drew a little arrow to the sofa.

The words blurred suddenly, and he let the pencil drop behind the sofa. He lay back down. Hammerman was in his mind again, and he closed his eyes. He tried hard to think of the days when he and Ezzie had been ready to handle crocodiles and bulls, quicksand and lions. It seemed a long time ago.

Betsy Byars, *The Eighteenth Emergency*

Puzzles

Australian bush fire

In this account of a bush fire all the sections except the first have been jumbled up. Write down the numbers in the correct order.

The air smelt of danger – the heat drew out a strong odour of eucalyptus, and the wind was scorching. Radio, press and television announced a day of acute fire danger.

At mid-morning a curl of grey smoke rose from the valley below. We learnt later that a youth lit the fire deliberately to demonstrate his fire-fighting prowess. We watched that smoke and the direction of the wind anxiously, and gathered our most important documents into a satchel.

1   The car jolted and the roof rack fell in our path. The precious seconds we lost then almost spelt our death. The fire front had reached the bottom of our garden, only 215 feet away. We abandoned the case on the bare earth. But when we returned only the handles were left.

    The fire swept on to new victims, and we circled back on the main road, expecting to view the ashes of the house.

2   In less time than it takes to tell, the fire roared 1,600 feet up the mountain and cut off the only road out. Burning leaves were falling faster than we could put them out.

3   Grass and shrubs burst into flame like a giant cracker on either side of the road a few feet from the car.

    And that rushing wall of flame, reaching high above the tops of the trees, was tearing uphill at about 40 miles an hour.

    We struck downhill on a mud track. For fully two weeks I was struck numb by the absolute horror of that moment.

4   The car stood on the road, ready for flight. We cleared fallen leaves from the guttering round the roof, filled the water pump, shut all doors and windows, and packed our suitcase.

    There was nothing to see, but suddenly I heard an ominous roaring and crackling.

5   We had our lives, and the loss of all but the clothes we wore seemed unimportant.

    A miracle had happened. As well as our lives, we had the bonus of a house unscathed.

The Times: 12th February 1967

Word study

These words all occur in this unit. The number after each one tells you the page it is on.

demolished 52	detonated 57
dazed 53	chaotic 58
suffocation 54	severed 59
regularly 54	sagged 61
muffled 56	awning 61

1 Find each word and read the sentence it is in.
2 Write each word on a new line.
3 Against each one write what you think it means. If you do not know, have a guess.
4 Look *all* the words up in the dictionary.
5 Write the correct meanings of any that you got wrong.

Headline news

Sometimes newspaper headlines are ambiguous: they can have more than one possible meaning. When this happens you have to read the story to work out what the headline means.

Choose one of these headlines and write two completely different newspaper reports or stories that could follow it. Try to make your stories short and interesting.

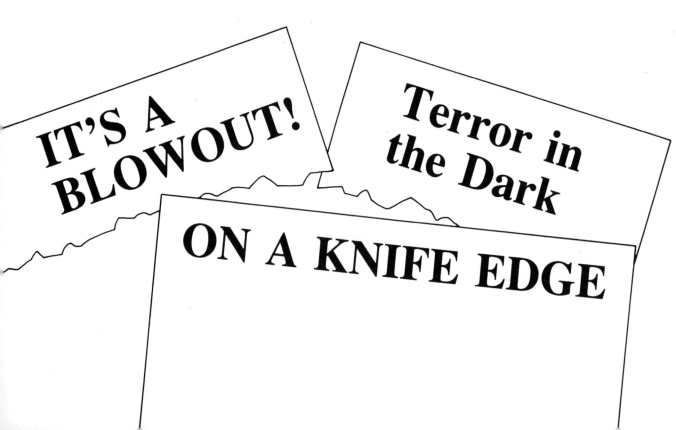

FRIENDS
and
ENEMIES

Which of these people do you think would be friendly?
Which might be unfriendly?
Can you tell whether people are friendly from their faces?

Enemies . . . or friends?

I was standing at the end of the lower playground and annoying Mr Samuels, who lived in the house just below the high railings. Mr Samuels complained once a week that boys from the school threw apples and stones and balls through his bedroom window. He sat in a deck chair in a small square of trim garden and tried to read the newspaper. I was only a few yards from him. I was staring him out. He pretended not to notice me, but I knew he knew I was standing there rudely and quietly. Every now and then he peeped at me from behind his newspaper, saw me still and serious and alone, with my eyes on his. As soon as he lost his temper I was going to go home. Already I was late for dinner. I had almost beaten him, the newspaper was trembling, he was breathing heavily, when a strange boy, whom I had not heard approach, pushed me down the bank.

I threw a stone at his face. He took off his spectacles, put them in his coat pocket, took off his coat, hung it neatly on the railings, and attacked. Turning round as we wrestled on the top of the bank, I saw that Mr Samuels had folded his newspaper on the deck chair and was standing up to watch us. It was a mistake to turn round. The strange boy rabbit-punched me twice. Mr Samuels hopped with excitement as I fell against the railings. I was down in the dust, hot and scratched and biting, then up and dancing, and I butted the boy in the belly and we tumbled in a heap. I saw through a closing eye that his nose was bleeding. I hit his nose. He tore at my collar and spun me round by the hair.

'Come on! come on!' I heard Mr Samuels cry.

We both turned towards him. He was shaking his fists and dodging about in the garden. He stopped then, and coughed, and set his panama straight, and avoided our eyes, and turned his back and walked slowly to the deck chair.

We both threw gravel at him.

'I'll give him "Come on!"' the boy said, as we ran along the playground away from the shouts of Mr Samuels and down the steps on to the hill.

We walked home together.

Dylan Thomas, *Portrait of the Artist as a Young Dog*

Questions to think and talk about

1 Why did Dylan Thomas and the other boy stop fighting?
2 Why did they walk home together?
3 Would it be true to say that they had been enemies and then suddenly became friends?
4 Does it ever happen like that in real life?
5 Does it ever happen the other way round?

Writing

1 Mr Samuels writes a letter to the Headmaster complaining about Dylan Thomas' behaviour.
2 When the other boy gets home he has to explain to his mother why his nose is bleeding. Write their conversation.

Escape

During the Second World War Bill Alliston was a gunner in a
Halifax Bomber. In Spring 1944 his plane was shot down and Bill
was injured in the leg. Bill and two other members of the crew,
Maurice Steel and John Collar, parachuted to safety. They landed in
Northern France, which was occupied by the Germans. Bill and his
friends set out to find their way back to England. They could only
travel very slowly because of Bill's injured leg, and they travelled by
night to avoid the Germans. During the day they hid in woods and
farm buildings, getting as much rest as they could. In this way they
reached Paris.

At Soissons, east of Paris, they met Maurice and Genevieve
Dupuis. They looked after the airmen, giving them food and hiding
them from the Germans. For five weeks they nursed Bill back to
health. The three men lived in a shed behind the house. Every time
the German soldiers came near they had to run away, for they knew
that the Dupuis would be punished and even killed if they were
found out.

Meanwhile the French Resistance movement was planning an
escape route for the RAF men. They would be taken to Spain and
from there it would be much easier for them to get back to England.
So the men set off. They were taken across the Pyrenees, the
mountains which separate France and Spain. In June they reached
Spain.

Just after the airmen had left Soissons, the Germans raided the
Dupuis' house. It was obvious that someone had tipped them off.
They took Maurice Dupuis away with them. They questioned and
tortured him, but he would not tell them where the airmen had
gone or who had helped them. His silence cost him his life, for he
died as a result of the torture. If he had talked many members of
the Resistance would have been caught and killed. Even the RAF
escapers might have been stopped.

To this day Bill Alliston and his wife are grateful to the Dupuis.
They regularly visit Genevieve to show their gratitude to her and to
her dead husband. Bill also helped to start the RAF Escapers'
Society. This is a group of men who escaped from France and
Germany during the war. They collect money to help families
whose husbands and fathers helped RAF men to escape during the
war.

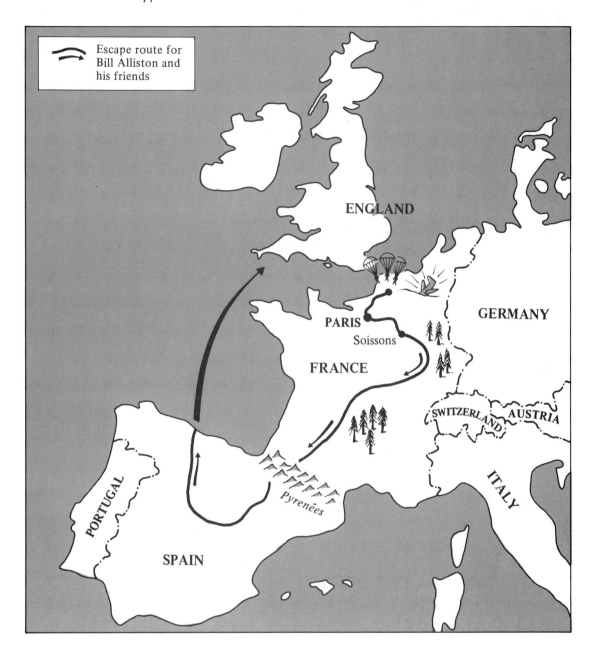

Questions

1. How many men survived the crash?
2. Where did they land?
3. What slowed them down as they travelled across country?
4. Who helped them in Soissons?
5. How long did it take for Bill's leg to get better?
6. What happened to Bill Alliston and Maurice Steel?
7. What did the Germans do to Maurice Dupuis?
8. What information did they want from him?
9. What do the Allistons still do?
10. What did Bill Alliston help to start?

The Bully Asleep

This afternoon, when grassy
Scents through the classroom crept,
Bill Craddock laid his head
Down on his desk, and slept.

The children came round him:
Jimmy, Roger, and Jane;
They lifted his head timidly
And let it sink again.

'Look, he's gone sound asleep, Miss,'
Said Jimmy Adair;
'He stays up all the night, you see;
His mother doesn't care.'

'Stand away from him children.'
Miss Andrews stooped to see.
'Yes, he's asleep; go on
With your writing, and let him be.'

'Now's a good chance!' whispered Jimmy;
And he snatched Bill's pen and hid it.
'Kick him under the desk, hard;
He won't know who did it.'

'Fill all his pockets with rubbish –
Paper, apple-cores, chalk.'
So they plotted, while Jane
Sat wide-eyed at their talk.

Not caring, not hearing,
Bill Craddock he slept on;
Lips parted, eyes closed –
Their cruelty gone.

'Stick him with pins!' muttered Roger.
'Ink down his neck!' said Jim.
But Jane, tearful and foolish,
Wanted to comfort him.

John Walsh

Friends

Friends be kept
Friends be gained
And even friends lost be friends regained
He had no foes he made them all into *friends*
A friend will die for you
Acquaintances can never make friends
Some friends want to be everybody's friend
There are friends who take you away from friends
Friends believe in friendship with a vengeance!
Some friends always want to do you favours
Some always want to get NEAR you
You can't do this to me I'm your friend.

Gregory Corso

Make friends, make friends,
Never, never break friends
Or you will catch the Flu
And that will be the end of you

Trad.

I fear it's very wrong of me,
And yet I must admit,
When someone offers friendship
I want the *whole* of it.
I don't want everybody else
To share my friends with me.
At least, I want *one* special one,
Who, indisputably,
Likes me much more than all the rest,
Who's always on my side,
Who never cares what others say,
Who lets me come and hide
Within his shadow, in his house –
It doesn't matter where –
Who lets me simply be myself,
Who's always, *always* there.

Elizabeth Jennings

What is a friend?

friend, girl-f., boy-f. 887 n. *loved one*; one's friends and acquaintances, acquaintance, intimate a.; lifelong friend, common f., friend's f.; gossip, crony, old c. (see *chum*); neighbour, good n., fellow-townsman, fellow-countryman; cater-cousin, clansman 11 n. *kinsman*; well-wisher, favourer, partisan, backer 707 n. *patron*; proxenus 660 n. *protector*; fellow, brother, confrère, partner, associate 707 n. *colleague*; ally, brother-in-arms 707 n. *auxiliary*; collaborator, helper, friend in need 703 n. *aider*; invitee, guest, welcome g., frequent visitor, persona grata; guest-friend, protegé; host, kind h. 882 n. *social person*; former friend, fair-weather f. 603 n. *tergiversator*.

close friend, best f., next f., near f.; best man, groomsman 894 n. *bridesman*; dear friend, good f., warm f., close f., fast f., firm f., loyal f.; intimate, bosom friend, friend of one's bosom, confidant, fidus Achates; alter ego, other self, shadow; comrade, companion, boon c., pot c.; good friends all, happy family; mutual friends, inseparables, band of brothers.

chum, gossip, crony; pal, mate, amigo, bully, bully-boy, buddy, bunkie, butty, side-kick; fellow, comrade, shipmate, messmate, room-mate, stable-companion 707 n. *colleague*; playmate, classmate, schoolmate, schoolfellow; pen-friend, pen-pal; hearties, my h.

Adj. *friendly*, non-hostile, amicable, well-affected, devoted 887 adj. *loving*; loyal, faithful, staunch, fast, firm, tested, tried 929 adj. *trustworthy*; fraternal, brotherly, sisterly, cousinly; natural, unstrained, easy, harmonious 710 adj. *concordant*; compatible, sympathetic, understanding; well-wishing, well-meaning, well-intentioned, philanthropic 897 adj. *benevolent*; hearty, cordial, warm, welcoming, hospitable 882 adj. *sociable*; effusive, demonstrative, back-slapping, hail-fellow-well-met; comradely, chummy, pally, matey; friendly with, well w., good friends w., at home w.; acquainted 490 adj. *knowing*; free and easy, on familiar terms, on visiting t., on intimate t., on the best of t.; intimate, inseparable, thick, thick as thieves, hand in glove.

Roget's *Thesaurus*

Man's best friend

Who is my neighbour?

And Jesus answering said, 'A certain man went down from Jerusalem to Jericho, and fell among thieves, which stripped him of his raiment, and wounded him, and departed, leaving him half dead. And by chance there came down a certain priest that way: and when he saw him, he passed by on the other side.

And likewise a Levite, when he was at the place, came and looked on him, and passed by on the other side.

But a certain Samaritan, as he journeyed, came where he was: and when he saw him, he had compassion on him.

And went to him, and bound up his wounds, pouring in oil and wine, and set him on his own beast, and brought him to an inn, and took care of him.

And on the morrow when he departed, he took out two pence, and gave them to the host, and said unto him, Take care of him; and whatsoever thou spendest more, when I come again, I will repay thee.

Which now of these three, thinkest thou, was neighbour unto him that fell among the thieves?

Gospel according to St Luke, *Authorized Version of the Bible*

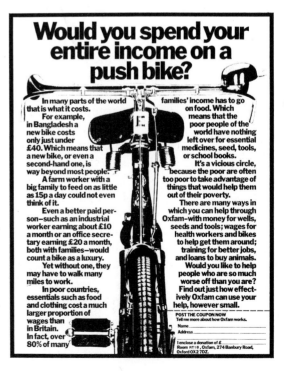

Kizzy

Diddakoi.
Tinker.
Tinkety-tink.
Gypsy, gypsy joker, get a red hot poker.
5 *Rags an' tags.*
Clothes pegs. Who'll buy my clothes-pegs?
    – only they said 'cloes-pegs'.
Who'll buy my flowers? – only they said 'flahrs'.
Diddakoi.

10 'If anyone,' said the teacher, Mrs Blount, in the classroom, 'any
one,' and her eyes looked sternly along the lines of tables filled with
boys and girls, 'teases or bullies or jeers at Kizzy Lovell, they will
answer for it to me.'
    Twenty-eight pairs of eyes looked back at Mrs Blount blandly
15 and innocently: 'As if we would,' they seemed to say. The twenty-
ninth pair, Kizzy's, looked down at her table; she had a curious
burning in her ears.
    'To me,' said Mrs Blount. 'We shall not have such behaviour in
this school.' But they would; silent and small, Kizzy knew that.
20   'Kizzy must be short for something,' Mrs Blount had asked
her, 'What is your real name, dear?'
    'Kizzy.'
    Mrs Blount had touched a sore spot; in Kizzy's family, as in
some gypsy clans, a child is given three names: a secret one
25 whispered by its mother the moment it is born and, when it is
grown, whispered again into the child's ear; a private or 'wagon'
name which is used only by its own people, and a third open name
by which it is known to the world. Kizzy seemed only to have one,
but that was because she was what they called her, a 'diddakoi', not
30 all gypsy. 'We don't say gypsies now. We say travellers,' Mrs
Blount told the children. Kizzy's father, pure Rom, had married an
Irish girl, but Kizzy looked gypsy to the children and they were half
fascinated, half repelled by her brownness and the little gold rings in
her ears – none of the other girls had golden ear rings. There was
35 one boy Kizzy liked, big Clem Oliver. 'I thought gypsies had black
eyes,' said Clem Oliver. 'Yours are dark dark brown. They're nice –
and these are pretty.' He touched the gold rings and Kizzy glowed
and, 'My Gran has gold sov'reigns for her ear rings,' she told Clem.
    'Never seen sov'reigns,' said Clem in awe. Clem made Kizzy

feel bigger, not small and frightened, big an' warm, thought Kizzy. Clem, though, was in an older class; she only saw him at break times, and the others teased. 'More than teased,' said Mrs Blount.

'But, Mildred, if you forbid people to do something, doesn't it usually make them want to do it even more?' asked Miss Olivia Brooke. Mrs Blount and her husband were lodging with Miss Brooke in the village until their own new house was built and had told her about Kizzy. 'Doesn't it?' asked Miss Brooke.

'Well, what would you have done?'

'Could you, perhaps, have interested them in the little girl? Made her romantic. Gypsies –'

'Travellers,' corrected Mrs Blount.

'I like the old name. Gypsies have a romantic side. If, perhaps, you had told them stories . . .' but Mrs Blount said she preferred to use her own methods and, 'I want you to give me your promise,' she told the class, 'that there will be no more teasing of Kizzy,' and she even asked them, child by child, 'Do you promise?'

'Mary Jo, do you promise?'

'Yes, Mrs Blount.'

'Prudence Cuthbert, do you?'

'Yes, Mrs Blount,' said Prue.

'Yes, Mrs Blount . . . Yes, Mrs Blount,' the answers came back, glib and meek – what Mrs Blount did not know was that every girl said it with her fingers crossed. Kizzy saw that from her seat at the back of the room and knew, as soon as Mrs Blount was out of the way, it would start again. *Tinker . . . diddakoi . . . gypsy joker . . . clothes pegs . . . old clothes . . .*

Kizzy had come to school in new clothes, or thought she had. Traveller women seldom buy new clothes from shops; they make them or beg them or buy them at country jumble sales, but hers had looked to Kizzy brand new; she loved the tartan skirt and red jersey, the school blue blazer all of them wore, white socks, but, 'Wearing Prue Cuthbert's clothes,' the girls jeered.

'They're mine,' said Kizzy.

'Now. They were Prue's. Prue's mum gave them for you.' Prudence Cuthbert was the worst of the girls and that night Kizzy had put the clothes down a hollow in one of the old apple trees full of dead leaves and water. Her grandmother had lammed her but Kizzy did not care; no one could wear them after that, and next day she wore her own clothes for school. It had never occurred to her, or her Gran, that they were peculiar clothes, but they looked most peculiar in class: a limp strawberry-pink cotton dress too long for her – her vest showed at the top – a brown cardigan that had been a boy's larger than Kizzy, but if she pushed the sleeves up it was not much too big; some of the buttons had come off but Gran had found

85 two large safety-pins. 'Where's your coat?' asked Mrs Blount.

'Don't need a coat.' Kizzy said it gruffly because she did not
have a coat and was afraid someone would give her one. She spoiled
the look of the school, 'and those clothes smell', said Prudence,
wrinkling up her nose. They did, but not of dirt. Gran washed them

90 often, hanging them along the hedge, while Kizzy wrapped herself
in a blanket; they smelled of the open air, of wood-smoke and a little
of the old horse, Joe, because she often hugged him.

'You live in a caravan?' asked Prue and, for the first time, she
sounded interested.

95 'In a wagon,' said Kizzy.

'It's a caravan. I seen it.'

'A wagon,' said Kizzy.

'In Admiral Twiss's orchard. He lets you but he's barmy.'

'He's not,' said Kizzy.

100 'He is. Everybody knows it. Barmy. Nuts.'

Prudence doubled up. Kizzy's hard small fist, hard as any
boy's, had hit her in the middle of her stomach.

Rumer Godden, *Diddakoi*

Puzzles

Who is my neighbour?

This is a modern version of the bible story printed on page 75.
Every seventh word has been missed out. Read the story through
carefully. Try to work out what you think each word should be.
Then write the number of each space and the word you think should
go there.

A man was going down the ....¹..... from Jerusalem to Jericho, and
fell ....²..... the hands of bandits. They tore ....³..... clothes off him
and beat him ....⁴...... Then they went and left ....⁵..... lying half-
dead on the road.

    ....⁶..... by accident, a priest was going ....⁷..... the same road.
He saw the ....⁸..... lying there, but he didn't stop. ....⁹..... went
on past him – on the ....¹⁰.... side of the road. It was ....¹¹.... the
same with a Temple caretaker. ....¹²...., too, came to the spot and
....¹³.... the man lying there; he, too, ...¹⁴.... not stop – he went
on past him on the other side of the ....¹⁵..... .

    Then a foreigner, who was on ....¹⁶.... journey across the
country, came upon ....¹⁷.... man. He saw him lying there,
....¹⁸.... felt very sorry for him. He ....¹⁹.... across to him, put
ointment ....²⁰.... his wounds and bandaged them up. He
....²¹.... him up onto the horse ....²².... had been riding, and
brought him ....²³.... an inn and looked after him.

    ....²⁴.... morning, he took a pound out ....²⁵.... his purse and
gave it to ....²⁶.... inn-keeper.

    'Look after him,' he said. '....²⁷.... it costs more than a pound,
....²⁸.... will put it right with you on ....²⁹..... way back.'

Alan T. Dale, *New World*

Word square

This word square contains eight words meaning friend. They all come from the list on page 74. How many can you find?

```
S  D  D  E  S  I  I  E  N  Y
A  C  O  M  R  A  D  E  F  F
I  R  H  E  N  I  D  I  P  E
N  I  T  O  S  R  P  U  A  L
R  Z  C  R  O  N  Y  I  L  L
F  X  L  Q  A  L  L  Y  Q  O
E  C  H  U  M  T  M  N  I  W
D  A  C  E  N  L  M  A  O  Y
I  O  D  L  O  N  S  U  T  F
N  P  A  R  T  N  E  R  G  E
```

Word study

All these words come from *Kizzy*.

innocently	sternly	awe
fascinated	clan	meek
lodging	repelled	blandly
gruffly	romantic	glib

1 Find each word and read the sentence it is in.
2 Write each word on a new line.
3 Against each one write what you think it means. If you do not
   know, have a guess.
4 Look *all* the words up in the dictionary.
5 Write the correct meanings of any that you got wrong.

MY HERO

Who are these people?
Is any of them *your* hero?
If you were to make a collection of heroes, whom would you include?

A brave man

On January 18th 1912, a group of explorers led by Robert Scott reached the South Pole. When they got there, they found that they had lost the race to be the first men to reach it. Another team, led by Amundsen, had beaten them to it. They began the return journey, but were hit by bad luck and bad weather. One member of the team, Titus Oates, became very weak.

Oates' feet were now badly frost-bitten and there is no doubt that the whole party was stricken with scurvy. Without the possibility of hot meals, Oates suffered more and more. Soon he realized that he could no longer pull the sledge. Inwardly he knew then what his fate was to be, but he was troubled by being a drag on the others. He spoke of this in confidence to Dr. Wilson, who could do no more than encourage him to try to keep going.

Scott, however, realized the situation perfectly clearly and ordered Wilson to hand out opium tablets so that each member of the party could die in the peace of sleeping if death became inevitable.

By March 15th Oates had reached the end of his tether. He could go no farther, but knew perfectly clearly that if he let his companions take up the extra burden of pulling him on the sledge they would have no hope at all. He begged to be left behind and die peacefully in his sleeping-bag, but neither Scott nor the other two would hear of it.

In his log Scott recorded: 'The surface remains awful, the cold intense and our physical condition running down. God help us. Not a breath of favourable wind for more than a week and apparently liable to head winds at any moment . . .

'Friday March 16th or Saturday 17th: Lost track of dates but think the last correct. Tragedy all along the line . . . Poor Titus Oates . . . was worse and we knew the end had come. Should this be found I want these facts recorded . . . We can testify to his bravery. He has borne intense suffering for weeks without complaint and to the very last was able and willing to discuss outside subjects. He did not – would not – give up hope until the very end. He was a brave soul . . . He woke in the morning – yesterday. It was blowing a blizzard. He said "I am just going outside and may be some time." He went out into the blizzard and we have not seen him since . . . We knew that poor Oates was walking to his death but though we tried to dissuade him we knew it was the act of a brave man and an English gentleman. We all hope to meet the end with a similar spirit, and assuredly the end is not far.'

Nevertheless, in recurrent blizzards and biting cold the three survivors staggered on.

Bowman, *From Scott to Fuchs*

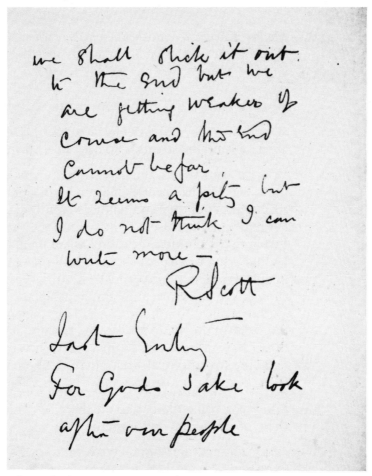

This is the last entry in Scott's diary.

Questions to think and talk about

1 On March 15th Oates wanted Scott and the others to leave him behind to die. They refused. Why do you think this was?
2 Were they right to refuse?
3 Oates walked out into the blizzard. What do you think of his action?
4 Many people believe that Scott and the others were *heroes*. What do they mean by the word *hero*?
5 Do you think they were heroes?
6 Can you think of any other people who have been heroes in this kind of way?

Writing

Think about the kind of person you believe to be a hero.
Think about the qualities he or she has that you admire.
Now write a story or a description about 'My Hero'.

A different kind of heroism

Mother Teresa was a teacher in a private school in Calcutta. She gave it up to care for the poor and dying in the city streets. Malcolm Muggeridge interviewed her.

MOTHER TERESA: In 1952 we opened the first Home for the Dying.

MALCOLM: When you say Home for the Dying, you mean that these are people on the streets who have been abandoned and are dying.

MOTHER TERESA: Yes, the first woman I saw I myself picked up from the street. She had been half eaten by the rats and ants. I took her to the hospital but they could not do anything for her. They only took her in because I refused to move until they accepted her. From there I went to the municipality and I asked them to give me a place where I could bring these people because on the same day I had found other people dying in the streets. The health officer of the municipality showed me an empty building; he asked me if I would accept it. Within twenty-four hours we had our patients there and we started the work of the home for the sick and dying who are destitutes. Since then we have picked up over twenty-three thousand people from the streets of Calcutta, of which about fifty per cent have died.

MALCOLM: What exactly are you doing for these dying people? I know you bring them in to die there. What is it you are doing for them or seeking to do for them?

MOTHER TERESA: First of all we want to make them feel that they are wanted, we want them to know that there are people who really love them, who really want them, at least for the few hours that they have to live, to know human and divine love. That they too may know that they are the children of God, and that they are not forgotten and that they are loved and cared about and there are young lives ready to give themselves in their service.

MALCOLM: What happens to the ones who don't die?

MOTHER TERESA: Those who are able to work we try to find some work for them, the others we try to send them to homes where they can spend at least a few years in happiness and comfort.

MALCOLM: You only want people who cannot get in anywhere else; for whom this is the last refuge, is that right?

MOTHER TERESA: Yes, the home is meant only for the street cases and cases that no hospital wants or for people who have absolutely no one to take care of them.

Malcolm Muggeridge, *Something Beautiful for God*

Questions		
	1	What did Mother Teresa give up to care for the dying?
	2	What did she do for the first dying woman she found?
	3	What did she ask the municipality for?
	4	How many people have she and the Sisters helped?
	5	What is the first thing they are trying to do for such people?
	6	Some do not die. How do the Sisters help them?
	7	Why don't the Sisters take these people to the hospitals?
	8	What does it mean to say that someone is *destitute*? If you do not know, use a dictionary to help you find out.
	9	What is a *refuge*?
	10	In what sense is Mother Teresa a *hero*?

Biggles and Ginger escape

Ginger delayed no longer. In the light of the torch he climbed on to the table, and then on the box that stood on it. This enabled him to reach the single large pane of glass above his head. He pushed it up, and allowed it to fall back gently on its hinges. A pull and he was through, lying flat, groping desperately for a hold on the sloping roof, aghast at what he saw. A few feet below him the roof ended in a black void. From other, similar holes of darkness rose the misshapen gables of ancient roofs, with here and there a gaunt chimney pointing like a black finger at the murky sky. What struck him at once was, Smith must have arranged his escape route in dry weather. He could have had no idea of what the old tiles would be like after rain. The roof might have been smeared with grease.

'Move along,' said a voice at his elbow, and twisting his face round, he saw Biggles beside him, replacing the skylight.

'Move along,' muttered Biggles. 'What are you waiting for?'

Ginger gasped. 'This is frightful,' he managed to get out. 'If I move, I shall slide off.'

'You can't spend the rest of your life where you are,' said Biggles tersely. 'Get weaving. If the police look through the skylight, they'll see us.'

The next five minutes to Ginger were something in the nature of a nightmare. Spreadeagled flat on the roof he inched his way along, fingers pressing against the tiles for any slight projection which might help him. Once a piece of moss came away in his hand and he thought he was gone; and he did in fact slide a little way before a protruding nail gave him respite. His eyes never left the chimney stack which was his objective. He thought he would never reach it. When he did, he clawed at it as a drowning man might clutch at a lifebelt; and there he clung, panting, striving to steady a racing heart, watching the black shape that he thought was Biggles making the dreadful passage. At the last moment, Biggles, too, started to slide; but with one arm round the chimney stack Ginger was able to give him a hand. For a nerve-shattering moment, Ginger feared that the whole stack would come crashing down under their combined weight as Biggles drew himself up. But then the immediate danger was past, and they both paused to recover from the shock of the ordeal.

'By thunder! That wasn't funny,' remarked Biggles, breathing heavily.

W. E. Johns, *Biggles Follows On*

To the rescue!

Can you work out what is happening in this story? What are they saying to each other?

In the daytime

In the daytime I am Rob Roy and a tiger
In the daytime I am Marco Polo
                 I chase bears in Bricket Wood
In the daytime I am the Tower of London
                 nothing gets past me
                 when it's my turn
                 in Harrybo's hedge
In the daytime I am Henry the fifth and Ulysses
                 and I tell stories
                 that go on for a whole week
                 if I want.
At night in the dark
                 when I've shut the front room door
                 I try and
                 get up the stairs across the landing
                 into bed and under the pillow
                 without breathing once.

Michael Rosen

The Rebel

When everybody has short hair,
The rebel lets his hair grow long.

When everybody has long hair,
The rebel cuts his hair short.

When everybody talks during the lesson,
The rebel doesn't say a word.

When nobody talks during the lesson,
The rebel creates a disturbance.

When everybody wears a uniform,
The rebel dresses in fantastic clothes.

When everybody wears fantastic clothes,
The rebel dresses soberly.

In the company of dog lovers,
The rebel expresses a preference for cats.

In the company of cat lovers,
The rebel puts in a good word for dogs.

When everybody is praising the sun,
The rebel remarks on the need for rain.

When everybody is greeting the rain,
The rebel regrets the absence of sun.

When everybody goes to the meeting,
The rebel stays at home and reads a book.

When everybody stays at home and reads a book,
The rebel goes to the meeting.

When everybody says, Yes please,
The rebel says, No thank you.

When everybody says, No thank you,
The rebel says, Yes please.

It is very good that we have rebels.
You may not find it very good to be one.

D. J. Enright

Adventures of Theseus

The road which led to the Isthmus was no more than a rough mule track, and the most dangerous spot was the bend at the foot of the Crane Mountain. Here the rocks rose very steeply, and on the left a precipice plunged down to the sea. Sometimes an avalanche of stones would block the path. Then the traveller had to climb down to the sea and walk along the narrow beach till it ended. After that he had to wade or swim to the place where he could climb up again to the mule track. Luckily for Theseus the path was clear today.

Soon he met a man with wild eyes and wild clothes sitting on a rock, with a bronze bowl full of water beside him. This was Skiron the brigand, and it was he who kept the path clear.

'You may not pass until you have paid me the toll,' said Skiron.

'I have no money,' said Theseus.

'You do not need money. You simply pay me by stooping to wash my feet in this bowl.'

'Is the sea-turtle hungry today, then?' said Theseus.

'What sea-turtle?' said Skiron angrily. 'I don't understand you.'

But he understood very well. As soon as a traveller stooped to wash his feet, he would kick him over the cliff into the sea, where a giant sea-turtle that ate nothing but men was swimming about, waiting to eat him.

'If you look over the cliff, you will see the turtle waiting,' said Theseus.

'And the moment my back is turned, you will push me over,' said Skiron. 'My wits are not as dim as you think. I tell you, there is no turtle there.'

'You are quite right,' said Theseus. 'Before I climbed up here, I went down to the water and cut off its head with my sword.'

'What!' said Skiron, and he turned and peered over the edge of the cliff.

At once Theseus picked up the bowl, hurled it at his head and knocked him over. Skiron turned six somersaults in the air and hit the water with a loud smack. A huge fountain of white spray rose into the air. When it had subsided, Theseus saw the giant sea-turtle break the surface and plunge down after Skiron for his last meal of human flesh.

Theseus was by now very tired, and, when some hours later he met a young man who offered him a bed for the night, he gladly accepted.

'My master Procrustes is most hospitable,' said the young man, 'and he loves to have a guest under his roof. He is lonely and enjoys hearing tales of foreign parts.'

'I am too tired to tell stories tonight,' said Theseus.

'They will keep till the morning. You shall have something to eat and then go straight to bed. My master's bed is famous – there is no other one like it in the world, for it fits every guest perfectly, no matter how tall or short he is. And you will sleep on it as you never slept before.'

It was almost dark when they came to a river. They were walking along the bank towards the bridge, when suddenly the servant missed his footing and fell in. He shouted for help, but the torrent quickly swept him away.

Theseus dropped his club and ran along the bank downstream till he saw him, thrashing about helplessly in the foaming water. He jumped in, seized him under the arms, and dragged him ashore.

To judge from his coughing and spluttering, the servant seemed to have swallowed half the river. When he had at last recovered his breath, he astonished Theseus by telling him that he must not on any account come to the house with him.

'Why not?' asked Theseus.

'Because you have saved my life, and now I want to save yours. If you lie down on my master's bed, you will never wake up again. If you are too long for it, he will lop off your legs till they are short enough; if you are too short, he will stretch your limbs till they are long enough. He treats all his guests in this way. I am the only one who fitted the bed exactly and he has kept me as his servant ever since. Hurry now and go back the way you came.'

But it was too late for Theseus to go back even if he had wanted to, for a lantern came bobbing towards them in the darkness, and the man who was carrying it was Procrustes. He had heard his servant shouting for help and had come out to see what was the matter.

'I fell into the torrent and this stranger saved me,' the servant explained.

'I shall be glad to reward him with a meal and a good night's rest,' said Procrustes. 'And while he's asleep, we can dry his clothes by the fire.'

'He is in a hurry to get to Corinth,' said the servant.

But Procrustes would take no refusal. He gripped Theseus by the arm and brought him to his house, which was just over the bridge. It was built of rough-hewn stones, and a wild fig-tree grew by the door. Inside a log fire was blazing – there was no other light in the room – and there was a sheep roasting on the spit and jugs of wine on the table.

While the servant prepared the meal, Procrustes and Theseus sat down at the table and sipped the wine. Theseus looked at his host's blue gown and all the gold and silver bracelets on his arms and wondered how many travellers like himself he had robbed and killed. Then he glanced over his shoulder and saw among the shadows the two wooden posts at the foot of the famous bed.

They ate the meal in silence, and when it was over Procrustes said, 'You must be very tired after your journey.' And he showed him the bed.

'It looks too long for me,' said Theseus.

'I will make sure that it fits you,' said Procrustes. 'Just lie down and you'll see.'

'I hate sleeping in wet clothes,' said Theseus. 'I thought you said you would dry them for me.'

'Ah yes, so I did. I will fetch you a tunic,' said Procrustes.

While he was gone from the room to fetch the tunic, Theseus had a word with the servant, who was busy clearing the table. Then he undressed, and when Procrustes brought in the tunic, he put it on and lay down on the bed.

At once Procrustes seized his ankles and fastened them with leather straps to the posts at the foot of the bed. Meanwhile the servant, who knew what to do, tied each wrist with a strap and fastened them – or, rather, pretended to fasten them – to posts at the head of the bed. When Procrustes, on his way to attend to the stretching-gear, was within reach, Theseus grabbed him round the waist with both arms and shouted to the servant to cut the straps on his feet. Next moment they were wrestling together in the firelight, while on the walls and the ceiling their shadows wrestled like black giants. They knocked over the table. They hurtled into a wine jar and smashed it, and the red wine poured over the floor. Theseus was a natural wrestler, and he soon had Procrustes at his mercy. With the servant's help he laid him on the bed and tied him down. As Procrustes fitted the bed exactly, there was no need to saw off his legs or use the stretching-gear. Instead he cut off his head with his sword and dragged the body outside for the wolves to devour. Then the servant spread two sheepskins on the floor near the fire, and they lay down and slept. They would not go near the bed.

So it was that Theseus, by his strength and skill and courage, freed the road to Athens of its terrors.

Ian Serraillier, *The Way of Danger*

Puzzles

Biggles and Ginger again

The story on page 86 continues like this. Every seventh word has been missed out. Read the story through carefully and try to work out what you think each word should be. Then write the number of each blank and the word you think should go there.

Slowly and with infinite care Biggles ....¹..... himself erect and put a hand ....²..... the chimney-pot. It came out ....³..... the rope which, yard by yard ....⁴..... withdrawn. Ginger guided the loose end ....⁵..... the edge of the gable, from ....⁶.....the chimney was an extension. What ....⁷..... below he could not see, but ....⁸..... to Smith there was a flat ....⁹...... . He stared down, but the starlight ....¹⁰.... dim with mist or cloud, and ....¹¹.... could see nothing distinctly.

Biggles made ....¹².... running knot round the chimney. 'Down ....¹³.... go,' he ordered.

The rest was ....¹⁴....,. Ginger went hand over hand down ....¹⁵.... rope and soon found himself on ....¹⁶.... flat surface. The relief, after the ....¹⁷.... was almost overwhelming. Biggles appeared beside ....¹⁸.... , and brought the rope down with ....¹⁹.... thud. They coiled it, picked it ....²⁰.... , and advanced cautiously until another pool ....²¹.... gloom appeared. Still nothing could be ....²².... distinctly, but below them was obviously ....²³..... yard of the scrap-metal merchant.

....²⁴..... was a little delay while a ....²⁵..... to which the rope could be ....²⁶..... was found. Then Ginger went down, ...²⁷.... stumble with a clatter on a ....²⁸.... of junk.

'Do you have to ....²⁹.... so much noise?' muttered Biggles shortly, ...³⁰.... he joined him.

'Sorry but I ....³¹.... see in the dark,' answered ....³².... coldly, wiping filthy hands on his ....³³.... .

Biggles buried the rope under a ....³⁴..... of rubbish. Then he looked at ....³⁵..... watch. 'Five minutes to go,' he ....³⁶...... . 'This way.'

How many words?

How many different words can you make out of the letters in:

SUPERMAN

You can only use each letter once in any word.

Crossword

Copy this crossword and then complete it. Some of the answers to the clues are to be found in this unit. If so, the page number is given.

Across
1 What the rebel would prefer to a dog. (89)
6 Mother . . . (85)
9 A word that can sometimes be used instead of 'and' to join two sentences.
10 Old-fashioned word that means 'before'.
11 Hero on page 86.

Down
2 The hat that lost its head.
3 In Roman numerals it is X.
4 A kind of hero, though some don't think so. (89)
5 A brave man and an English gentleman. (82)
7 Certain.
8 Comes before Roy on page 88.

Word study

These words all occur in this unit. The number after each one tells you the page it is on.

inevitable 82
intense 82
murky 86
protruding 86

hospitable 90
torrent 91
rough-hewn 91

1 Find each word and read the sentence it is in.
2 Write each word on a new line.
3 Against each one, write what you think it means. If you do not know, have a guess.
4 Look *all* the words up in the dictionary.
5 Write the correct meanings of any that you got wrong.

BANK RAID

The raid

broke
nion
Poli
...
he Jus-
aid it
injunc-
, due to

es are
m strik-
Reagan
down
of the
the air
walked

our fares, Our drivers try to be helpful with customer inquiries."

STOP PRESS

A bank clerk was shot this afternoon in a raid on a London Bank. It is believed that the gang – two men and two women – escaped in a waiting car with at least half a million pounds.

Writing You are the reporter who has to write the full story of the robbery for the next edition of the paper.

1 Decide on the full details of the raid:
   a when and where it took place
   b the name and address of the injured man
   c how old he is
   d any other information about him
   e exactly what happened in the raid
   f why the clerk was shot
   g any details of the getaway car

2 Make up a headline for the story.

3 Write the story for the paper.

Wanted

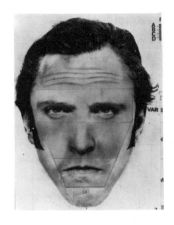

The policeman in charge of the investigation is Chief Superintendent Johnston. When he arrives at the bank he interviews the bank staff and the customers who were in the bank when the raid took place. When he interviews Mrs Andrews, the chief cashier, she describes one of the robbers like this:

'One of them was very tall. He must have been at least 6′ 5″. He had broad shoulders and he was heavily built. His hair was thin and greasy. It was a mousy-brown colour. He had long sideboards. He was clean shaven. He was wearing a leather jacket and blue jeans.'

Here is the photo-fit picture the police made from Mrs Andrews' description.

Writing

1 Mrs Andrews can also remember quite a lot about the other members of the gang. Write down what she said about them. Use the pictures on page 95 and the information on page 96 to help you. You can write in one of these forms:

straight description
direct speech (check on page 174)
script (check on page 172)

2 Make up 'Wanted' posters for two members of the gang (with sketches or photo-fit pictures if you wish). An example is shown below.

WANTED

Steven Jennings is 27 years old, 5′ 10″ tall, slim built. He has blue eyes and extensive scarring on the right side of his body.

Will disguise his appearance and adopt convincing fake identities.

Police records

After talking to everyone at the Bank, Chief Superintendent Johnston goes to Scotland Yard to look at the files in the Criminal Records Office. He finds two files which might be useful. One seems to fit the tall man Mrs Andrews described:

```
Brian John ROWLANDS

Born: 20.10.46
Age: 35
Place of Birth: Weybridge, Surrey
Height: 6' 3"
Weight: 210lb.
Identification Marks:
A scar on his left shoulder.
Status: Married.  2 children.


Previous Criminal Record
1960  Convicted of breaking and entering.  Let off with a warning.
1963  Convicted of mugging.  Sent to Borstal for 2 years.
1970  Convicted of burglary.  Sent to Wormwood Scrubs for 3 years.
1975  Sent for trial for armed robbery.  Case dismissed through lack
      of evidence.

Last known address: 30 Bridge Street,
                    Greenwich,
                    London  S.E.10

Last known job: Fork-lift truck driver
```

This file also includes:

ROWLANDS, Brian John					
RIGHT HAND	THUMB	1	2	3	4

Mrs Joan Rowlands, 3 George St., Weybridge, Surrey. Mother	'I have not seen Brian for nearly three years. He was never in trouble as a young boy. Things started to go wrong when his father died in 1959. He seemed to stop working at school then and went out every evening. He mixed with bad company, that was the problem.'
Richard Smart, 15 Bridge St., Greenwich, London S.E.10. Neighbour	'He was a good neighbour. Sometimes we would not see him for a few days, and we would wonder where he had gone. He never said much about himself, you see, and he was not the sort of man who liked you being nosy. But if you ever needed anything fixed, then it was Brian you went to see.'
John Stone, 2 Victor Rd., Croydon. Warehouse Manager	'Brian Rowlands worked in my warehouse for six months. Then he suddenly disappeared. He was reliable and he worked hard. He used to keep himself to himself. Every now and then he would have a nasty argument with someone. I suppose he had a quick temper really.'

Writing   File 2. Chief Superintendent Johnston has found *two* files. The second one seems to fit one of the people that Mrs Andrews described and you wrote about. Make up an official file for this second person. Include in it the three documents illustrated for Rowlands. Add any other papers you think might be there.

Hostage

It is two days after the robbery. A policeman sees a man who looks like Rowlands walking along the road. When challenged, the man (who *is* Rowlands) pulls out a gun. He fires at the policeman, but misses, and runs to his car. As this is happening, you and a friend appear on the scene. Rowlands grabs you as hostages and drives off with you in his car.

He takes you to a deserted dockland area where he is hiding with the rest of the gang:

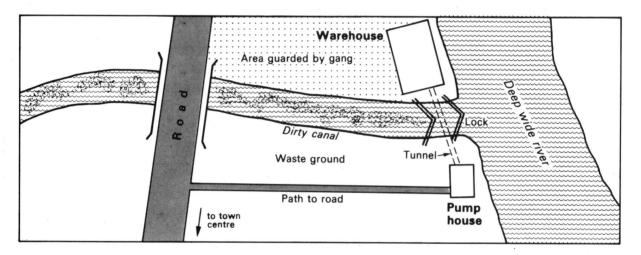

The gang tie you up and shut you up on the top floor of the warehouse. Then they barricade themselves in the warehouse. The police surround the area as it begins to get dark.

The river is too dangerous to swim. The gang can see (and shoot at) the area between the warehouse and the road. There is a secret tunnel between the cellar of the warehouse and a deserted pump house. But you are on the top floor of the warehouse.

Instructions Decide the following points:
a How you escape from the warehouse.
b What you do when you have escaped.
c How the police find out where the gang are.
d How the gang are captured.

Writing Tell the story of what happens. Finish at the point where the gang is taken away by the police to be questioned.

Search

The gang is captured and taken to the police station. Later Chief Superintendent Johnston and his men search the warehouse. They find documents and other objects that convince them that the men they have arrested are the gang who robbed the bank.

Instructions   Decide the following points:
    a What the police are looking for.
    b What they find to link the men with the robbery.

Writing   You are Chief Superintendent Johnston. Write your report. Describe what you find. Include drawings of any documents (e.g. passports, maps, driving licences) that you find.

Trial

Three months later, the gang members are brought to trial. These are the main characters involved in the trial.

The defendants   the gang members who are being tried.

Prosecuting counsel   the lawyer who has to prove that they are guilty.

Defence counsel   the lawyer who has to prove that they are innocent.

Witnesses   people who saw the bank robbery; police who investigated it; anyone else who can provide evidence.

Judge   he controls the trial; advises the jury about the law; and sums up the evidence for them.

Jury   twelve men and women who listen to all the evidence and then decide if the defendants are guilty or innocent.

This is the order in which things happen:

1 **The charge**   the defendants are told what crime(s) they are accused of. They plead 'Guilty' or 'Not guilty'.

2 **The prosecution**   the prosecuting counsel tries to prove that the defendants are guilty. He calls witnesses to give evidence to prove his case. These witnesses can be questioned ('cross-examined') by the defence counsel.

3 **The defence**   the defence counsel then tries to prove that the defendants are innocent. He calls witnesses. These may be cross-examined by the prosecution.

4 **The summing-up**   the judge sums up the evidence for the jury.

5 **The verdict**   the jury go away to a separate room and try to make up their minds. At least ten of them must agree. When they have decided, they go back into the court room. Their foreman tells the judge their verdict.

6 **The sentence**   if the defendants are guilty, the judge then sentences them to a period in prison. They are taken away. If they are innocent they are set free.

Writing   Write the story of the trial of the gang. Write it in one of these forms:
a   as a play
b   as a newspaper report
c   as a diary written by one of the people involved in the trial

What is the girl doing?
Who is the old man?
Why is he on the cliffs?
What happens next?

DISCOVERING

103

Mission: earth

The flying saucer came down vertically through the clouds, braked to a halt about fifty feet from the ground, and settled with a considerable bump on a patch of heather-strewn moorland.

'That,' said Captain Wyxtpthll, 'was a lousy landing.' He did not, of course, use precisely these words. To human ears his remarks would have sounded rather like the clucking of an angry hen. Master Pilot Krtclugg unwound three of his tentacles from the control panel, stretched all four of his legs, and relaxed comfortably.

'Not my fault the automatics have packed up again,' he grumbled.

'Oh, all right! We're down in one piece, which is more than I expected. Tell Crysteel and Danstor to come in here. I want a word with them before they go.'

Crysteel and Danstor were, very obviously, of a different species from the rest of the crew. They had only one pair of legs and arms, no eyes at the back of the head, and other physical deficiencies which their colleagues did their best to overlook. These very defects, however, had made them the obvious choice for this particular mission, for it had needed only a minimum of disguise to let them pass as human beings.

'Now you're perfectly sure,' said the Captain, 'That you understand your instructions?'

'Of course,' said Crysteel, slightly huffed.

'Good. And the language?'

'Well, that's Danstor's business, but I can speak it reasonably fluently now. It's a very simple language and after all we've been studying their radio programmes for a couple of years.'

'Any other points before you go?'

'Er – there's just one matter.' Crysteel hesitated slightly. 'It's quite obvious from their broadcasts that the social system is very primitive, and that crime and lawlessness are widespread. Many of the wealthier citizens have to use what are called "detectives" or "special agents" to protect their lives and property. Now we know it's against regulations, but we were wondering . . .'

'What?'

'Well, we'd feel much safer if we could take a couple of Mark III disrupters with us. Remember that radio play I was telling you about? It described a typical household, but there were two murders in the first half hour!'

'Oh, very well. But only a Mark II – we don't want you to do too much damage if there is trouble.'

'Thanks a lot; that's a great relief. I'll report every thirty minutes as arranged. We shouldn't be gone more than a couple of hours.'

Captain Wyxtpthll watched them disappear over the brow of the hill. He sighed deeply.

Samuel Higginsbotham was settling down to a snack of cheese and cider when he saw the two figures approaching along the lane. He wiped his mouth with the back of his hand, put the bottle carefully down beside his hedge-trimming tools, and stared with mild surprise at the couple as they came into range.

'Mornin',' he said cheerfully between mouthfuls of cheese.

The strangers paused. One was surreptitiously ruffling through a small book which, if Sam only knew, was packed with such common phrases and expressions as: 'Before the weather forecast, here is a gale warning,' 'Stick 'em up – I've got you covered!', and 'Calling all cars!' Danstor, who had no needs for these aids to memory, replied promptly enough.

'Good morning my man,' he said in his best BBC accent. 'Could you direct us to the nearest hamlet, village, small town or other such civilized community?'

'Eh?' said Sam. He peered suspiciously at the strangers, aware for the first time that there was something very odd about their clothes. One did not, he realized dimly, normally wear a roll-top sweater with a smart pin-striped suit of the pattern fancied by city gents. And the fellow who was still fussing with the little book was actually wearing full evening dress which would have been faultless but for the lurid green and red tie, the hob-nailed boots and the cloth cap. Crysteel and Danstor had done their best, but they had seen too many television plays.

Arthur C. Clarke, *Of Time and Stars*

Questions to think and talk about

1 How have Crysteel and Danstor prepared for their exploration on earth?
2 Why does Crysteel want a Mark III disrupter – and what do you imagine it does?
3 What sort of person is Samuel Higginsbotham?
4 How does he feel about the two visitors?
5 Do you think that Crysteel and Danstor are likely to be successful explorers?
6 How do you think their expedition will end?

Writing

Crysteel and Danstor visit your school. Describe what happens – *either* as if it was being described later by Danstor, or as told by you, describing what *you* saw.

The discovery of lysozome

Alexander Fleming was trying to find out how to kill the bacteria that cause disease. He used to grow different types of bacteria on glass dishes to learn more about them. He was not a tidy man and his bench was always littered with papers and old dishes that he had finished with. He never threw away any of these old dishes without looking at them very carefully first.

One day Fleming came across to Dr Allison, his colleague, with a dish in his hand.

'This is very interesting,' he said.

On the dish were growing certain bacteria. It was an old dish and it should have been covered evenly with germs. Instead there were a number of patches where there were hardly any at all. In fact it looked as though the germs in these patches were dying off.

Fleming's notes showed him that he had put a drop of mucus from his own nose onto this dish. He had a cold and he wanted to see if there were any organisms in the mucus that were causing his heavy catarrh.

Something in the mucus from his nose was killing off the germs on the dish. Was he at last on the track of a solution to the problem of curing infectious diseases?

A good deal of the moisture in the nose comes from tears. They overflow from the eyes after they have been used to keep them moist and clean. So Fleming now tried the effects of tears on some bacteria growing in broth in a test-tube. The vast numbers of germs in the broth made it look cloudy. But within five or six seconds of adding a few tears, the broth became completely clear. The tears killed the germs.

Fleming named the substance in tears *lysozome*. He did further experiments on it. Unfortunately they showed that lysozome killed harmless germs much more easily than dangerous ones. Still, Fleming had made a great discovery. Lysozome was a natural antiseptic, nature's first defence against microbes. And he had discovered it by accident.

antiseptic   a. & n. (substance) destroying or preventing growth of the bacteria that cause disease and decay.

bacterium   n. (pl. *bacteria*) microscopic single-celled organism occurring in large numbers, some types causing decay and disease.

catarrh   n. inflammation of mucous membrane, esp. of nose.

disease   n. unhealthy condition; (particular) illness or disorder.

germ   n. part of organism capable of developing into new one; rudiment, elementary principle; microbe.

microbe   n. micro-organism, esp. bacterium causing disease (*not in scientific use*).

mucous   a. secreting, covered by, mucus. **mucous membrane** inner surface-lining of hollow organs of body **mucus** n. sticky substance secreted by and usu. protecting mucous membrane.

Questions   Answer each of these questions by writing a complete sentence. Do not copy whole sentences from the story.
1   What was Fleming trying to do?
2   What kind of person was he?
3   What did he find in an old dish?
4   What had he done to the dish earlier on?
5   What did he do next?
6   What happened then?
7   What had Fleming discovered?

Writing   You are a newspaper reporter at the time when Fleming discovered lysozome. Write a report of his discovery, under this headline:

NATURE'S OWN CURE
Wonderful discovery by British scientist

Your editor has told you that there is only space in the paper for 100 words.

Who are you?

A : Where were you yesterday evening?
B : What do you mean?
A : Where were you?
B : When?
A : Between seven o'clock and half past nine.
B : What's it got to do with you?
A : I'll ask the questions, if you don't mind.
B : Who are you . . . and what do you want?
A : The truth – that's what I want.
B : But I've got nothing to hide.
A : Good. Then in that case you can answer the question. Where were you last night?
B : Well . . . I er . . .
A : And what were you doing?
B : I was . . . I was at home. Yes. That's where I was.
A : At home.
B : Yes. Watching television.
A : Prove it.
B : Look, don't you believe me?
A : Can you prove it?
B : Look, what is this?
A : In other words you can't prove it.
B : Who are you? And what right have you to ask me all these questions?
A : All right then. We'll start from the beginning. Fill in this form.

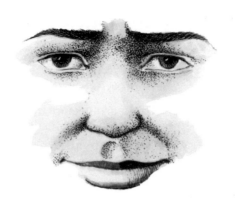

P/27/82401

PCF 27

SURNAME:

OTHER NAMES:

FULL ADDRESS:

TELEPHONE:

DATE OF BIRTH:

PLACE OF BIRTH:

NAME OF PARENT OR GUARDIAN: WEIGHT:

HEIGHT:

COLOUR OF HAIR:

COLOUR OF EYES:

OTHER DISTINGUISHING FEATURES:

Discovering the back yard

The ground out in the backyard was made of a kind of coarse concrete, full of tiny shells and pebbles – shingle from our sands. The little stones, worn smooth by the pounding of the North Sea breakers, had been made even smoother by the passage of countless colliers' boots and housewives' shoes. The stones were mostly brown in colour, but there were also yellow and black and white and striped ones, and others that were the brown-blue shade of a ripe black eye; there were also well-rubbed fragments of old brick, and bits of green, dull bottle-glass, both pale and dark. These, with jagged portions of broken shells, were all conglomerated in a hard, smooth, cement-roughened mass that looked dull when dry but shone and sparkled when it rained or when my father or Mr Battey 'scrubbed the yard' – a weekly ritual – with great pailfuls of tap-water and a stiff-bristled yard broom. I had soon noticed, on the beach, how stones and shells and seaweed shone when they were wet, and how disappointingly dull they were when dry. Our backyard was like having a section of the beach on our own scullery doorstep – but fixed, and hard, and immovable, despite the great tides of tap-water my father regularly sluiced over it.

Among all these variegated pebbles there was one that stood out. It was in a dark corner of the yard, near Mrs Battey's green-painted coal-house door. This pebble was slightly smaller than the rest, but it was bright scarlet. It was the only one of its kind, and its brilliant red had earned it the name of 'The Bloodstone.'

Many were the tales and prohibitions it inspired. Some said it was the tooth out of a Chinese donkeyman's head, and others that a coalman had spat it out, red-hot. Some said it was a 'bogle.' Now on Tyneside a 'bogle' was something one picked out of one's nose, but it could also be something spooky. Romantic-minded little girls said it was a queen's finger-nail, and indeed it had the shape and size of a delicate little finger-nail. But the boys of course scoffed at this idea. Some said it was a scarlet bean, that sprouted diamonds once every hundred years. Some swore it was giant's blood. But all were agreed that it was fatal to stand on it, or to touch it, unless you had spat on it first. If you were to touch it without spitting on it, you would drop down dead, or your finger would fall off.

James Kirkup, *The Only Child*

Accidentally

accidentally
broke a teacup –
reminds me
how good it feels
to break things

Ishakawa Takuboku

Poems of Solitary Delights

What a delight it is
When, of a morning,
I get up and go out
To find in full bloom a flower
That yesterday was not there.

What a delight it is
When, skimming through the pages
Of a book, I discover
A man written of there
Who is just like me.

What a delight it is
When everyone admits
It's a very difficult book,
And I understand it
With no trouble at all.

What a delight it is
When I blow away the ash,
To watch the crimson
Of the glowing fire
And hear the water boil.

What a delight it is
When a guest you cannot stand
Arrives, then says to you,
'I'm afraid I can't stay long,'
And soon goes home.

Tachibana Akemi

The island

Mafatu is a South-Sea-Island boy. He has left his home on the island of Hikueru and travelled across the sea by canoe. His canoe has been wrecked in a storm and Mafatu injured. He struggles to the shore and collapses.

There was a fan of light spreading in the east. Mafatu stirred and opened his eyes. For a moment he lay there motionless in the cool mosses, forgetful of the events which had cast him up on this strange shore. Then it all came crowding back upon him, and he scarcely dared to believe that there was earth, solid earth beneath him; that once more Moana, the Sea God, had been cheated. He struggled to sit upright, then fell back upon one elbow. Uri lay close at hand, holding a robber-crab in his forepaws, cracking the tough shell and extracting the meat with gusto. There was Kivi, too, with his beak tucked back under his wing in sleep. Kivi, who had led his friends to this island . . .

Mafatu pulled himself to a sitting position. The action called for more strength than he realized. He was giddy with thirst and there was an odd weakness in his limbs. His right leg was swollen and painful. He remembered then that he had banged it against the coral when the canoe struck. He discovered that there was a gash on his calf; he must take care of it, for coral wounds were poisonous.

The chuckle of the cascade reached his ears and made him aware of a stabbing need of water. He plunged his face into the pool and drank deeply. Then, prompted more by instinct than by conscious thought, he withdrew, to let the water run down his swollen throat sparingly, with caution. Its cool magic stole through his tissues, bringing with it new life and restoring force. He sighed, and sank back on the mossy bank, relishing the strength that quickened his tired body. Soon he must find food . . . There were thousands of coconut trees on every hand, rich with green fruit; but Mafatu was not yet strong enough to climb. Later he would try it. Then he would make fire, too; and he must search the island to find out if it were inhabited; and there was a shelter to build. Oh, there was much to do! He hardly knew where to begin. But now it was enough just to lie there and feel strength returning, to know that he was safe from the sea. The sea . . . He shuddered. Maui, God of the Fishermen, had carried him safely across the ocean currents.

'Uri,' the boy muttered thickly, 'we're alive! It wasn't all a bad dream. It really happened.'

The answering wag of his dog's tail was further assurance of reality. As Mafatu's brain cleared of cobwebs, a sudden thought brought him up swiftly: this silent island was not Tahiti. What island was it then? Did it . . . oh! did it belong to the black eaters-of-men? Were they even now watching him from secret places in the jungle, biding their time? He glanced about in apprehension. But the solitude was unbroken save for the soft cooing of ghost-terns and the gentle plash of the cascade.

On his left hand, far offshore, the reef boomed to the charging surf; the curve of the beach reached out like two great arms to enclose the lagoon. Coconuts and pandanus trooped in shining legions to the very edge of the sea. A flight of green and purple parakeets flashed across the sky and vanished. There was no other sign of life. No voices of men; no laughter of children; no footprint in the sand.

The volcanic peak that formed the background of the island rose perhaps three thousand feet straight up out of the sea. It was the cone of a volcano long extinct. From its base ridges of congealed lava flowed down to the distant shore. Once, in the dim beginnings of the world, this mountain had belched forth fire and brimstone, spreading destruction over the land. But the forgiving jungle through fertile centuries had crept back up the slopes, clothing them in green, green.

The boy rose and stood stretching his stiff limbs. The water had restored him and he felt much stronger. But he found that the earth heaved with the sea's own motion, and he swayed to keep his balance. His leg still pained, and he would need the juice of limes to cauterize the coral wound, and *purau* leaves to make a healing

bandage. Near by was a tree loaded with wild limes. He plucked half a dozen of the fruits, broke them on a bit of coral, and squeezed the juice into the wound. He winced as the caustic stung; but when he had bound on the leafy bandage with a twist of vine, it seemed that already his leg felt better. Soon the swelling would be gone.

Close at hand he discovered a rude trail made by wild pigs and goats in their wanderings across the mountain. The trail led up through the foothills to a high plateau which, the boy decided, would make a splendid lookout. From that point of vantage he would be able to survey his entire island and the sea for a distance of many miles.

He followed the path where it led back into the jungle, along the course of the swift-flowing stream. The trail sloped up sharply and Mafatu pulled himself up by roots and trailing lianas, now climbing, now crawling flat on his stomach. He found that he had to stop every now and then to catch his breath. Uri ran beside him, dashing off on this scent and that; the dog's shrill, sharp bark shattered the morning stillness.

For a quarter of a mile the coconuts held, beautiful trees that were more luxuriant than any in Hikueru. It was always thus in the rich soil of the volcanic islands. Then came a belt of breadfruit and wild bananas, of oranges and guavas and mangoes. The roots of the *mapé* trees – the island chestnut – twisted over the ground in strange, tormented shapes. Vines trailed like aerial ropes from the high branches where orchids bloomed, while little parakeets fled on swift wings and vanished in the green gloom. Mafatu had never before seen woods like these, for Hikueru was open and wind-swept. These endless legions of trees seemed to close in upon him, imprison him with reaching arms, with heady odours, with eerie light and shadow. Ferns grew higher than a tall man's head; the roof of leaves was powdered with starry blossoms.

By the time Mafatu reached the plateau he was exhausted and his leg throbbed with pain. He lay down full length upon the volcanic rock and watched wild goats leaping from peak to peak high above his head and heard their shrill bleating in the clear air. When he caught his breath he sat up again and looked about. The plateau appeared to divide the island into halves. From his vantage point the boy could see its whole circumference. He was hoping desperately for some sign of human habitation, yet fearing it too; for who knew whether humans might prove friends or enemies? He almost hoped that the island were uninhabited, but if it were – He shivered as he realized his isolation. Even at sea in his small canoe he had not felt so utterly alone as he did here on this strange, high island. Everything about it was alien and forbidding.

Armstrong Sperry, *The Boy Who Was Afraid*

Puzzles

Discovering the news

In this passage some of the words have been left out. Read the story and try to work out what you think the words should be. Then write down the number of each blank and the word that you think should go there.

A rich landowner was returning home ....¹..... a journey when he met by ....²..... side of the road the steward ....³..... had left in charge of his ....⁴..... while he was away.

'Ah, steward,' ....⁵..... the returning gentleman cheerily, how are ....⁶...., old fellow? And how are things ....⁷..... home?'

'Bad enough, sir,' said the ....⁸...... 'The magpie is dead.'

'Well, well,' ....⁹..... the gentleman. 'Gone at last, eh? ....¹⁰.... did he die?'

'Over-ate himself, ...¹¹...... '

'Did he indeed! The greedy bird! ....¹².... was it he liked so much?'

'....¹³..... . That's what got him, sir. Horseflesh.'

'....¹⁴.... !' said the landowner. 'However did ....¹⁵.... manage to find so much horseflesh ....¹⁶.... it killed him?'

'All your father's ....¹⁷.... , sir.'

'What! My father's horses! Are ....¹⁸..... dead too?'

'Aye, sir. Died of ....¹⁹..... .'

'Why ever should they be overworked, ...²⁰..... ?'

'Carrying all that water, sir.'

'Carrying ....²¹..... ! What were they carrying water for, ...²²..... ?'

'For sure, sir, to put the ....²³..... out.'

'Fire! What fire?'

'Why, sir, ...²⁴.... fire that burned your father's house ....²⁵.... the ground.'

'Good Lord, steward, is ....²⁶.... father's house burnt down? How did ....²⁷.... happen?'

'I reckon it were the ....²⁸.... , sir.'

'What torches?'

'Them we used ....²⁹.... your mother's funeral, sir.'

'My mother ....³⁰.... dead?'

'Aye, poor lady. She never ....³¹.... up after it.'

'After what, man, ...³².... what?'

'The loss of your father, ...³³..... .'

'My father? Dead, too?'

'Yes, poor ....³⁴.... . Took to his bed as soon ....³⁵.... he heard of it.'

'Heard of ....³⁶.... ?'

'Of the bad news, sir.'

'More ....³⁷.... news! What bad news?'

'Well, sir, ...³⁸.... bank has failed and all your ....³⁹.... is lost, and you're not worth ....⁴⁰.... penny in the world, sir. I ....⁴¹.... I'd come and wait on you ....⁴².... tell you about it, sir, for ....⁴³.... thought you'd like to hear the ....⁴⁴.... .'

Aidan Chambers, *Funny Folk*

Word puzzle

Copy the puzzle and then complete it. If you fill in the answers to all the clues, you will find out the key word.

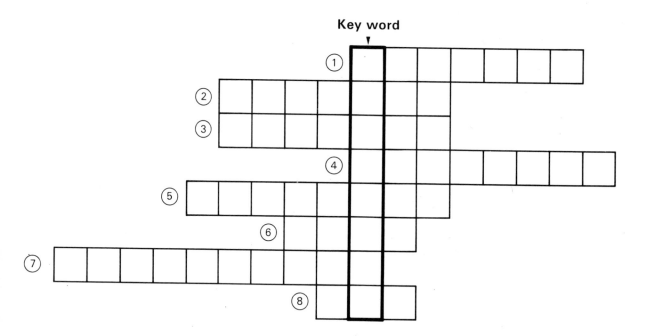

Clues

1 The earth explorer who spoke to Sam. (p. 105)
2 The scientist who discovered lysozome. (p. 106)
3 His colleague. (p. 106)
4 The earth explorer who wanted to be armed. (p. 104)
5 Nature's own cure. (p. 106)
6 Mafatu's seagull friend. (p. 112)
7 James Kirkup's special stone. (p. 108)
8 Mafatu's dog. (p. 112)

There have always been men who wished they could fly like the birds. Why do you think this is?

If you could fly, where would you go, and what would you do?

Which of these aeroplanes would be most interesting to fly, and why?

   jet fighter   glider   supersonic airliner

If you had the chance, would you go hang gliding?

Icarus

The ancient Greeks had a story, or 'myth', about man's wish to fly.

The famous inventor Daedalus was once the prisoner of King
Minos. Daedalus had been working for the king on the island of
Crete. He had invented many wonderful things and the king was
very pleased. At last Daedalus decided he wanted to go back to his
home in Greece, with his son Icarus. When he told King Minos this,
the king refused. He said that he would keep Daedalus and Icarus
prisoner on the island. He made sure that they could not escape by
boat. It was too far to swim, so all seemed lost.

Daedalus realized that the only way they could escape from the
island was to fly. He collected together wax and string and feathers.
Then he set to work. With his simple materials he made two sets of
wings: one for Icarus and one for himself.

When the wings were finished, he fitted one pair onto Icarus'
arms and explained to him how to use them.

'You must take care,' he said. 'Do not fly too high, or the heat
of the sun will melt the wax. Do not fly too low, or the sea will wet
the feathers and you will drown.' Then he put on his own wings and
launched himself into the air. 'Follow me closely!' he called.

Icarus did as he was told. At first he found it difficult and tiring
to beat his wings. Gradually it became easier. Soon they had left the
island and were flying over the sea. Icarus felt the rush of air through
his wings and was excited. So this was flying! He found that he
could soar up high and then swoop low. He quickly forgot all his
father's advice. Higher and higher he went, soaring up towards the
sun. At last he went so high that the heat of the sun began to melt
the wax on his wings. As soon as he realized what was happening,
he tried to go lower, but it was too late. The feathers began to
separate and the wings fell apart. Icarus dropped into the sea like a
stone, and was drowned.

At first Daedalus did not realize what had happened. Believing
that his son was following him he flew on towards Greece. Finally
he looked back and saw that Icarus was no longer behind him. He
turned back at once. After a short time he saw feathers floating on
the surface of the water. He swooped down as low as he dared and
then he saw the body of his son rise to the surface. With a heavy
heart, Daedalus raised the body of his son from the sea and carried it
away. He took it to a nearby island, where, with many tears, he
buried it. In memory of his son, he named the island Icaria – the
island of Icarus.

Questions to think and talk about

1. Why didn't Icarus do as his father told him?
2. Do you think his father was asking him to take too big a risk?
3. Whose fault was it that Icarus died?

Writing

1. What was Icarus thinking at different times in the story?
   Write down what he might have been thinking at these times:
   a. When his father told him about the plan to escape.
   b. As the wings were fitted on.
   c. When he began to fly.
   d. When the wax began to melt.

2. Write a story or a poem about being able to fly. Choose your own title or write about this one:

   My First Flight

3. Invent a man-powered flying machine, serious or funny. Make a detailed drawing of your invention and write a description of how it works.

4. Suppose you had the chance to meet and talk to the pilot of the hang glider in the picture on page 117. Make a list of the questions you would like to ask him. Then write down the conversation as a script. (Look at *Script* on page 172 to see how to do this.)

The flight of the Sedge Warbler

Sedge Warblers spend the summer in Britain and Europe. In the autumn they fly south to West Africa. There they spend the winter.

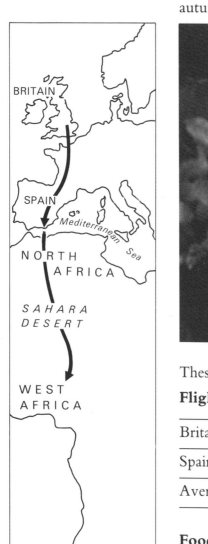

These are some of the facts about their migration flight.

Flight stages

Britain to southern Spain = 1,600 km	
Spain to West Africa = 2,400 km	
Average speed = 40 kph	

Food and weight
1 Sedge Warblers normally weigh 10½ grams.
2 Before the flight they stock up with food. Their weight almost doubles.
3 When they reach southern Spain they have lost about 4½ grams.
4 When they reach West Africa they weigh about 10 grams.
5 If their weight goes below 9½ grams, they die.
6 Many die on the journey.

True or false?
According to the information on the facing page, some of the following statements are true, some are false, and for some it is impossible to tell. Read them carefully and check them against the passage. Then for each one write down:

true
or false
or impossible to tell.

1 Sedge Warblers are migratory birds.
2 They only migrate from Britain.
3 They spend the winter in south-west Africa.
4 The first stage of their journey ends in Spain.
5 The total distance they cover is 2,400 kilometres.
6 The total distance they cover is 4,000 miles.
7 It takes them about 60 hours to travel from southern Spain to West Africa.
8 When they reach Spain they weigh about one and a half times their normal weight.
9 Between Spain and West Africa they lose about 10 grams.
10 When they leave Britain they weigh about 20 pounds.
11 Many die in the Sahara desert.
12 Sedge Warblers fly from West Africa to Britain and Europe every year.

Writing
1 Suppose your younger sister or brother asked you what 'migration' means. Write a short explanation that someone of, say, seven years old would understand.
Note: you may need to do some research in a dictionary or encyclopaedia before you can do this properly.
2 *Flight Towards the Sun*: write the story of the Sedge Warbler's journey south, as told by one of the birds.
3 *The Great Summer Migration*: a Martian visits England and observes our behaviour. He observes that at summer weekends and especially during July and August, Earthmen migrate into the country and to the sea. He writes a scientific report on his observations of this human migration.

Flying

These pictures show the stages of movement as a bird lands on a nest.

The Snow Goose

In the late spring of 1930 Philip Rhayader came to an abandoned lighthouse at the mouth of the Aelder. He lived there and worked there alone the year round. He was a painter of birds and of nature who had withdrawn from all human society. He was a hunchback and his left arm was crippled, thin and bent at the wrist, like the claw of a bird.

    One November afternoon, three years after Rhayader had come to the Great Marsh, a child approached the lighthouse studio by means of the sea wall. In her arms she carried a burden.

She was desperately frightened of the ugly man she had come to see, for legend had already begun to gather around Rhayader, and the native wild-fowlers hated him for interfering with their sport.

    But greater than her fear was the need of that which she bore.
5 For locked in her child's heart was the knowledge, picked up somewhere in the swampland, that this ogre who lived in the lighthouse had magic that could heal injured things.

She had never seen Rhayader before and was close to fleeing in panic at the dark apparition that appeared at the studio door, drawn by her footsteps – the black head and beard, the sinister hump, and the crooked claw.

She stood there staring, poised like a disturbed marsh bird for instant flight.

But his voice was deep and kind when he spoke to her.

'What is it, child?'

She stood her ground, and then edged timidly forward. The thing she carried in her arms was a large white bird, and it was quite still. There were stains of blood on its whiteness and on her kirtle where she had held it to her.

The girl placed it in his arms. 'I found it, sir. It's hurted. Is it still alive?'

'Yes. Yes, I think so. Come in, child, come in.'

Rhayader went inside, bearing the bird, which he placed upon a table, where it moved feebly. Curiosity overcame fear. The girl followed and found herself in a room warmed by a coal fire, shining with many coloured pictures that covered the walls, and full of a strange but pleasant smell.

The bird fluttered. With his good hand Rhayader spread one of its immense white pinions. The end was beautifully tipped with black.

Rhayader looked and marvelled, and said: 'Child, where did you find it?'

'In t' marsh, sir, where fowlers had been. What – what is it, sir?'

'It's a snow goose from Canada. But how in all heaven came it here?'

The name seemed to mean nothing to the little girl. Her deep violet eyes, shining out of the dirt of her thin face, were fixed with concern on the injured bird.

She said: 'Can 'ee heal it, sir?'

'Yes, yes,' said Rhayader. 'We will try. Come, you shall help me.'

There were scissors and bandages and splints on a shelf, and he was marvellously deft, even with the crooked claw that managed to hold things.

He said: 'Ah, she has been shot, poor thing. Her leg is broken, and the wing tip, but not badly. See, we will clip her primaries, so that we can bandage it, but in the spring the feathers will grow and she will be able to fly again. We'll bandage it close to her body, so that she cannot move it until it has set, and then make a splint for the poor leg.'

Her fears forgotten, the child watched, fascinated, as he worked, and all the more so because while he fixed a fine splint to

the shattered leg he told her the most wonderful story.

The bird was a young one, no more than a year old. She was
born in a northern land far, far across the seas, a land belonging to
England. Flying to the south to escape the snow and ice and bitter
cold, a great storm had seized her and whirled and buffeted her
about. It was a truly terrible storm, stronger than her great wings,
stronger than anything. For days and nights it held her in its grip
and there was nothing she could do but fly before it. When finally it
had blown itself out and her sure instincts took her south again, she
was over a different land and surrounded by strange birds that she
had never seen before. At last, exhausted by her ordeal, she had sunk
to rest in a friendly green marsh, only to be met by the blast from
the hunter's gun.

'A bitter reception for a visiting princess,' concluded Rhayader.
'We will call her "La Princess Perdue", the Lost Princess. And in a
few days she will be feeling much better. See!' He reached into his
pocket and produced a handful of grain. The snow goose opened its
round yellow eyes and nibbled at it.

The child laughed with delight, and then suddenly caught her
breath with alarm as the full import of where she was pressed in
upon her, and without a word she turned and fled out of the door.

Paul Gallico, *The Snow Goose*

The Red Cockatoo

Sent as a present from Annam –
A red cockatoo.
Coloured like the peach-tree blossom,
Speaking with the speech of men.
And they did to it what is always done
To the learned and eloquent.
They took a cage with stout bars
And shut it up inside.

Po Chu-I (*translated by Arthur Waley*)

When Birds Remember

Birds scattered in a treetop cheeping twitting
clucking twitching fluttering
twittering squeaking scratching
chirping whistling fluttering
flitting
rustling fidgeting
pecking trilling

SUDDEN
SILENCE

Birds in a tight
cloud flying off
on an important
errand they had
almost forgotten about.

Robert Froman

The Ostrich

The ostrich roams the great Sahara.
Its mouth is wide, its neck is narra.
It has such long and lofty legs,
I'm glad it sits to lay its eggs.

Ogden Nash

The Sparrowhawk

Wings like pistols flashing at his sides,
Marked, above the meadow runaway tides,
Galloping, galloping with an easy rein.
Below, the field mouse, where the shadow glides,
Holds fast the purse of his life, and hides.

Russell Hoban

The Eagle

He clasps the crag with crooked hands;
Close to the sun in lonely lands,
Ring'd with the azure world, he stands.

The wrinkled sea beneath him crawls;
He watches from his mountain walls,
And like a thunderbolt he falls.

Alfred, Lord Tennyson

Making a paper kite

Modern hang gliders like the one at the beginning of this unit were developed from kites. A designer who had a big influence on them was Francis Rogallo. He invented a flexible kite, which had no sticks or spars. This is a version of it you can make with stiff paper.

You need: a sheet of stiff A4 paper, thread, sticky tape.

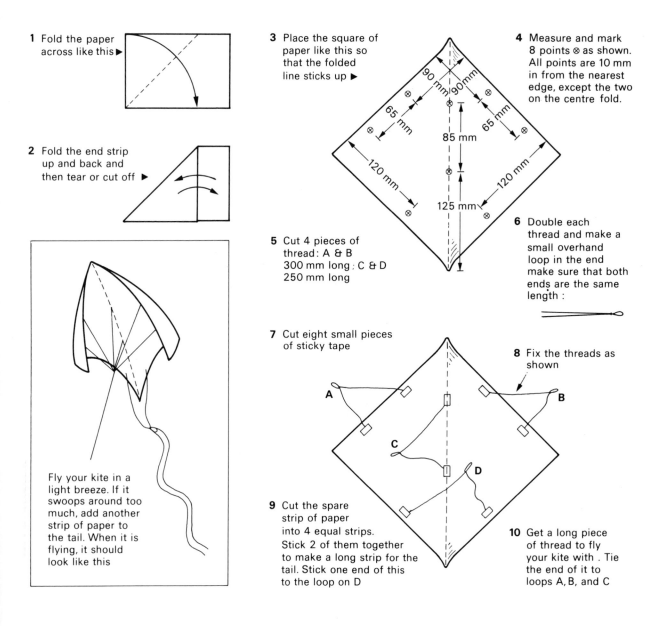

1 Fold the paper across like this ▶

2 Fold the end strip up and back and then tear or cut off ▶

3 Place the square of paper like this so that the folded line sticks up ▶

4 Measure and mark 8 points ⊗ as shown. All points are 10 mm in from the nearest edge, except the two on the centre fold.

90 mm 90 mm
65 mm 65 mm
85 mm
120 mm 120 mm
125 mm

5 Cut 4 pieces of thread: A & B 300 mm long ; C & D 250 mm long

6 Double each thread and make a small overhand loop in the end make sure that both ends are the same length :

7 Cut eight small pieces of sticky tape

8 Fix the threads as shown

A   B

C   D

9 Cut the spare strip of paper into 4 equal strips. Stick 2 of them together to make a long strip for the tail. Stick one end of this to the loop on D

10 Get a long piece of thread to fly your kite with . Tie the end of it to loops A, B, and C

Fly your kite in a light breeze. If it swoops around too much, add another strip of paper to the tail. When it is flying, it should look like this

Puzzles

The kite

In this story all the sentences except the first are in the wrong order. Write the numbers in the correct order. Then write three or four more sentences to finish the story.

Last Christmas Ginnie was given a kite.

1 She tightened it up and began to run into the wind.
2 She put the kite together and tied on the string.
3 With a *Crack!* the string broke.
4 On Boxing Day there was a good wind so she decided to try it out.
5 Suddenly there was an extra-strong gust of wind.
6 Walking backwards she let out the string.
7 Ginnie was so excited.
8 She went to the park all alone.
9 Higher and higher it went.
10 Then she put the kite down on the ground.
11 Soon the kite was rising into the air.

Bird puzzle

The names of twelve different birds are hidden in this puzzle. They may go across, downwards, or diagonally up or down.

```
O T H R U S H I S H Z Q
C P I T O R P E N F T E
H A T A N K H A I D O N
A S S C D U C K R I L T
F W E D T L Y I O R N E
F A A U E A B N N R O I
I L G E O K Y N C T S W
N L U A C R O O K R W C
C O L A W C S E A Z A R
H W L D R O B I N D N O
M B S T A R L I N G D W
C O N U Y E T U O N S R
```

Make a list of all the names you can find.

Word study

These words all occur in this unit. The number after each one tells you the page it is on.

supersonic 117	lofty 126
soar 118	pinions 124
swoop 118	primaries 124
migration 120	eloquent 126
trilling 126	

1 Find each word and read the sentence it is in.
2 Write each word on a new line.
3 Against each one, write what you think it means. If you do not know, have a guess.
4 Look *all* the words up in a dictionary.
5 Write the correct meanings of any that you got wrong.

Crossword

Some of the answers to this crossword are to be found in this unit. If so, the page number is given.

Across
1 The river near which Rhayader lived. (p. 123)
4 The surname of one of the poets on page 126.
6 A group of people who work or play together.
8 A fool . . . or a four-legged animal.
9 Something that birds and kites have (p. 128)

Down
2 Rhayader called the Snow Goose, 'The...........Princess'. (p. 125)
3 What the ostrich does in the Sahara. (p. 126)
4 Tidy.
5 What Rhayader wanted the Snow Goose's wing to do. (p. 124)
7 A word that means 'when' or 'because'.

STRANGE &
MYSTERIOUS

Who do you think these people are?
Where are they?
What do you think they are doing?
Why do you think they are doing it?

The ghost in the cupboard

When Laura said she had seen a ghost coming out of the clothes closet in the bedroom she had not meant to tell a lie. She really believed she had seen one. One evening, before it was quite dark and yet the corners of the room were shadowy her mother had sent her upstairs to fetch something out of the chest, and, as she leant over it, with one eye turned apprehensively towards the clothes closet corner, she thought she saw something move. At the time she felt sure she saw something move, though she had no clear idea of what it was that was moving. It may have been a lock of her own hair, or the end of a window-curtain stirring, or merely a shadow seen sideways; but, whatever it was, it was sufficient to send her screaming and stumbling downstairs.

At first, her mother was sorry for her, for she thought she had fallen down a step or two and hurt herself; but when Laura said that she had seen a ghost she put her off her lap and began to ask questions.

At that point the fibbing began. When asked what the ghost was like, she first said it was dark and shaggy like a bear; then that it was tall and white, adding as an after-thought that it had eyes like lanterns and she thought it was carrying one, but was not sure. 'I don't suppose you are sure,' said her mother dryly. 'If you ask me it's all a parcel of fibs, and if you don't look out you'll be struck dead, like Ananias and Sapphira in the Bible★,' and she proceeded to tell their story as a warning.

After that, Laura never spoke of the closet to anyone else but Edmund; but she was still desperately afraid of it, as she had been as long as she could remember. There was something terrifying about a door which was never unlocked, and a door in such a dark corner. Even her mother had never seen inside it, for the contents belonged to their landlady, Mrs Herring, who when she moved out of the house had left some of her belongings there, saying she would fetch them as soon as possible. 'What was inside it?' the children used to ask each other. Edmund thought there was a skeleton, for he had heard his mother say, 'There's a skeleton in every cupboard,' but Laura felt it was nothing as harmless.

After they were in bed and their mother had gone downstairs at night, she would turn her back on the door, but, if she peeped round, as she often did – for how otherwise could she be sure that it

★ Acts V 1-5

was not slowly opening? – all the darkness in the room seemed to be piled up in that corner. There was the window, a grey square, with sometimes a star or two showing, and there were the faint outlines of the chair and the chest, but where the closet door should have been was only darkness.

'Afraid of a locked door!' her mother exclaimed one night when she found her sitting up in bed and shivering. 'What's inside it? Only a lot of old lumber you may be sure. If there was anything much good, she'd have fetched it before now. Lie down and go to sleep, do, and don't be so silly!' *Lumber! Lumber!* What a queer word, especially when said over and over beneath the bedclothes. It meant odds and ends of old rubbish, her mother had explained, but, to her, it sounded more like black shadows come alive . . .

Flora Thompson, *Lark Rise to Candleford*

Questions to think and talk about	1 · What made Laura think there was a ghost?
	2 Why did she start to lie?
	3 Do you think she was silly?
	4 How did her mother behave when she said she had seen a ghost?
	5 Do you think this was the right way to treat Laura?
	6 What do you suppose Laura thought might be in the cupboard?
	7 Why are people afraid of the dark and of dark places?
	8 Are there such things as ghosts?

Writing

1 Laura's father wrote to Mrs Herring and asked if she could empty the cupboard so that they could use it:

'One day she arrived and turned out to be a little, lean old lady with a dark brown mole on one leathery cheek and wearing a black bonnet with jet dangles, like tiny fishing rods. Edmund and Laura sat on the bed and watched her . . .'

Tell the story of what happened when she opened the cupboard. Write it as if you were Laura.

2 Here is the beginning of a story. Write the rest of it.

Last summer we went to stay in the country. A friend of my uncle's lent us his house.

'Treat it just like your own home,' he said. 'Do what you like, with one exception. Never go into the little attic room at the top of the stairs.' One day when I was very bored I went exploring. I found myself at the top of the stairs by the door to the attic room. I tried the handle. To my surprise it turned easily and the door opened . . .

Extrasensory perception

It was April 9th 1912. A crowd of people stood on the dockside at Southampton. They were watching the splendid new liner, *Titanic*, steaming out of port. It was its maiden voyage. Suddenly a woman in the crowd pushed forward.

5 'That ship will sink!' she shouted. Her friends tried to calm her down. The *Titanic* was unsinkable, they said. It was built to the very latest design. Nothing could go wrong. But the woman would not be reassured.

'No!' she cried. 'They will all be drowned.' Five days later she
10 was proved right. The *Titanic* hit an iceberg and sank. About 1,500 people were killed.

This is an example of precognition, knowing what is going to happen in the future. Precognition is one form of extrasensory perception. Extrasensory perception, or ESP, is the ability to know
15 things without the use of your five senses.

There are other forms of ESP. Some people have the ability to know what you are thinking, without being told. We call this telepathy. Others can 'see' things that are actually hidden from them. They may know what is in a darkened room, or be aware of
20 things that are out of sight. This gift is known as clairvoyance. Perhaps the most exciting form of ESP is called psychokinesis. It is the ability to change or move objects just by thought. You may have seen or read about people who can, for example, bend spoons simply by the power of thought. That is psychokinesis.

25 Some of the things said about ESP may seem fantastic. Scientists in America and Russia, however, take ESP very seriously. They believe that it may be useful in any future war between their countries. They are studying it very carefully.

Questions
1 Where did the *Titanic* sail from on its first voyage?
2 Why was the woman upset?
3 What did her friends tell her?
4 Why did the *Titanic* sink?
5 What does precognition mean?
6 How many kinds of ESP are there?
7 What is another word for mind-reading?
8 Why are American and Russian scientists studying ESP?

Writing
1 If you could have ESP, which kind would you choose and why?
2 Write a story about a person who possesses the gift of either telepathy or psychokinesis.

Miller's End

When we moved to Miller's End,
   Every afternoon at four
A thin shadow of a shade
   Quavered through the garden door.

Dressed in black from top to toe
   And a veil about her head
To us all it seemed as though
   She came walking from the dead.

With a basket on her arm
   Through the hedge gap she would pass,
Never a mark that we could spy
   On the flagstones or the grass.

When we told the garden boy
   How we saw the phantom glide,
With a grin his face was bright
   As the pool he stood beside.

'That's no ghost-walk,' Billy said,
   'Nor a ghost you fear to stop –
Only old Miss Wickerby
   On a short cut to the shop.'

So next day we lay in wait,
   Passed a civil time of day,
Said how pleased we were she came
   Daily down our garden way.

Suddenly her cheek it paled,
   Turned, as quick, from ice to flame.
'Tell me,' said Miss Wickerby.
   'Who spoke of me and my name?'

'Bill the garden-boy.' She sighed,
   Said, 'Of course, you could not know
How he drowned – that very pool –
   A frozen winter – long ago.'

Charles Causley

Ghost hunt

HORROR AT GRANGE TOWERS

Mr David Hackett and his wife Hilary fled in horror last .night from their new home, Grange Towers. Strange sounds and human screams, flashing lights and an unearthly glowing presence drove them trembling from their new home.

Grange Towers has a history of hauntings. Ever since it was built, in 1878, there have been stories of ghosts and strange noises in the house. An earlier owner, Sir Arthur Pine, is said to have killed himself after spending a night alone in the dreaded West Tower. It was in the library, next to the West Tower, that Mr Hackett first heard unexplained noises, just over a week ago. Since then, he reports weird sounds and lights in the dining room and the North Tower as well. But it was in the lounge that late last night, he and

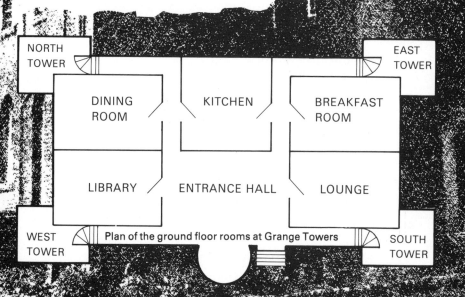

Plan of the ground floor rooms at Grange Towers

NORTH TOWER · EAST TOWER · DINING ROOM · KITCHEN · BREAKFAST ROOM · LIBRARY · ENTRANCE HALL · LOUNGE · WEST TOWER · SOUTH TOWER

Letter from the Society for Psychical Research to one of their members.

> and so we wondered if you would be prepared to carry out a full-scale investigation of recent happenings at Grange Towers.
>
> What we need is hard scientific evidence. If you are interested, please let me know and let me have a list of any equipment you need for this project.
>
> I enclose the Society's list of basic questions. As you know we ask these of anybody who claims to have seen a ghost. It might be a good idea if you call

Questions to be answered by those who believe that they may have seen or experienced a ghost

1 Could it have been an ordinary person, a shadow, a hanging coat, etc., or someone playing tricks?
2 If you heard ghostly sounds, could they have been normal – a cracking branch, birds, ordinary footsteps, your own breathing, wind in the chimney, or a hoax?
3 Has the place a reputation for haunting? If so, did you know, and were you expecting a ghost?
4 Why are you sure you weren't dreaming?
5 Did you recognize the apparition? If so, how?
6 Did anyone else see it before or afterwards without either knowing about the other's experience?
7 If anyone else was with you, did he see it? If he did, could the words you spoke have given him a clue to what you had seen?
8 If it was the apparition of a living person, were there any unusual features (e.g. clothes, behaviour) which you later found to be correct?
9 Did you or anyone else who saw it make a written record? If it foretold something – e.g. a death – did you write it down *before* the prophecy was fulfilled?
10 Have you had any other apparently psychic experiences? If so, how many and what kind?

Society for Psychical Research, P. Haining, *Ghosts, The Illustrated History*

Space haunting

The space-suits we use on the station are completely different from the flexible affairs men wear when they want to walk around on the moon. Ours are really baby spaceships, just big enough to hold one man. As soon as I'd settled down inside my very exclusive spacecraft, I switched on power and checked the gauges on the tiny instrument panel. All my needles were well in the safety zone, so I lowered the transparent hemisphere over my head and sealed myself in. For a short trip like this I did not bother to check the suit's internal lockers, which were used to carry food and special equipment for extended missions.

It was at that moment I launched myself out into the abyss, that I knew something was horribly wrong.

It is never completely silent inside a space-suit; you can always hear the gentle hiss of oxygen, the faint whirr of fans and motors, your own breathing – even, if you listen carefully enough, the rhythmic thump that is the pounding of your own heart. These sounds are the unnoticed background of life in space, for you are aware of them only when they change.

They had changed now; to them had been added a sound which I could not identify. It was an intermittent, muffled thudding, sometimes accompanied by a scraping noise, as of metal upon metal.

I froze instantly, holding my breath and trying to locate the alien sound within my ears. The meters on the control board gave no clues; all the needles were rock-steady on their scales, and there were none of the flickering red lights that would warn of impending disaster. That was some comfort, but not much. I had long ago learned to trust my instincts in such matters; their alarm signals were flashing now, telling me to return to the station before it was too late . . .

It was no longer possible to pretend that the noise disturbing me was of some faulty mechanism. Though I was in utter isolation, far from any other human being, I was not alone. The soundless void was bringing to my ears the faint but unmistakable stirrings of life.

In that first heart-freezing moment it seemed that something was trying to get into my suit – something invisible, seeking shelter from the cruel and pitiless vacuum of space. I whirled madly in my harness, scanning the entire sphere of vision around me. There was nothing there, of course. There could not be – yet that purposeful scrabbling was clearer than ever.

Despite the nonsense that has been written about us, it is not true that spacemen are superstitious. But can you blame me if I suddenly remembered how Bernie Summers had died, no farther from the station than I was at this very moment?

It was one of those 'impossible' accidents; it always is. Three things had gone wrong at once. Bernie's oxygen regulator had run wild and sent the pressure soaring, the safety valve had failed to blow – and a faulty joint had given way instead. In a fraction of a second, his suit was open to space.

I had never known Bernie, but suddenly his fate became of overwhelming importance to me – for a horrible idea had come into my mind. One does not talk about these things, but a damaged space-suit is too valuable to be thrown away, even if it has killed its wearer. It is repaired, renumbered – and issued to someone else . . .

What happens to the soul of a man who dies between the stars, far from his native world? Are you still here, Bernie, clinging to the last object that linked you to your lost and distant home?

As I fought the nightmares that were swirling around me – for now it seemed that the scratchings and soft fumblings were coming from all directions – there was one last hope to which I clung. For the sake of my sanity I had to prove that this wasn't Bernie's suit – that the metal walls so closely wrapped around me had never been another man's coffin.

It took me several tries before I could press the right button and switch my transmitter to the emergency wave-length. 'Station,' I gasped. 'I'm in trouble! Get records to check my suit history and –'

I never finished; they say my yell wrecked the microphone. But what man alone in the absolute isolation of a space-suit would *not* have yelled when something patted him softly on the back of the neck?

Arthur C. Clarke, *Of Time and Stars*

How do you think this story ends?

Flannan Isle

'Though three men dwell on Flannan Isle
To keep the lamp alight,
As we steered under the lee, we caught
No glimmer through the night.'

A passing ship at dawn had brought
The news, and quickly we set sail,
To find out what strange thing might ail
The keepers of the deep-sea light.

The winter day broke blue and bright
With glancing sun and glancing spray
While o'er the swell our boat made way,
As gallant as a gull in flight.

But as we neared the lonely Isle
And looked up at the naked height,
And saw the lighthouse towering white
With blinded lantern, that all night
Had never shot a spark
Of comfort through the dark,
So ghostly in the cold sunlight
It seemed that we were struck the while
With wonder all too dread for words.

And, as into the tiny creek
We stole beneath the hanging crag,
We saw three queer black ugly birds –
Too big by far in my belief,
For cormorant or shag –
Like seamen sitting bolt-upright
Up on a half-tide reef:
But, as we neared, they plunged from sight
Without a sound or spurt of white.

And still too mazed to speak,
We landed; and made fast the boat;
And climbed the track in single file,
Each wishing he was safe afloat
On any sea, however far,
So it be far from Flannan Isle:
And still we seemed to climb and climb
As though we'd lost all count of time

And so must climb for evermore.
Yet, all too soon, we reached the door –
The black, sun-blistered lighthouse-door,
That gaped for us ajar.

As, on the threshold, for a spell
We paused, we seemed to breathe the smell
Of limewash and of tar,
Familiar as our daily breath,
As though 'twere some strange scent of death;
And so yet wondering, side by side
We stood a moment still tongue-tied;
And each with black foreboding eyed
The door, ere we should fling it wide
To leave the sunlight for the gloom:
Till, plucking courage up, at last
Hard on each other's heels we passed
Into the living-room.

Yet, as we crowded through the door
We only saw a table, spread
For dinner, meat and cheese and bread;
But all untouched; and no one there:
As though, when they sat down to eat,
Ere they could even taste,
Alarm had come; and they in haste
Had risen and left the bread and meat,
For at the table-head a chair
Lay tumbled on the floor.
We listened, but we only heard
The feeble chirping of a bird
That starved upon its perch;
And, listening still, without a word
We set about our hopeless search.
We hunted high, we hunted low,
And soon ransacked the empty house;
Then o'er the Island, to and fro
We ranged, to listen and to look
In every cranny, cleft or nook
That might have hid a bird or mouse:
But though we searched from shore to shore
We found no sign in any place,
And soon again stood face to face
Before the gaping door,
And stole into the room once more
As frightened children steal.

Ay, though we hunted high and low
And hunted everywhere,
Of the three men's fate we found no trace
Of any kind in any place
But a door ajar, and an untouched meal,
And an overtoppled chair.

And as we listened in the gloom
Of that forsaken living-room –
A chill clutch on our breath –
We thought how ill-chance came to all
Who kept the Flannan Light,
And how the rock had been the death
Of many a likely lad –
How six had come to a sudden end
And three had gone stark mad,
And one whom we'd all known as friend,
Had leapt from the lantern one still night,
And fallen dead by the lighthouse wall –
And long we thought
On the three we sought,
And on what might yet befall.

Like curs a glance has brought to heel
We listened, flinching there,
And looked, and looked, on the untouched meal,
And the overtoppled chair.

We seemed to stand for an endless while,
Though still no word was said,
Three men alive on Flannan Isle
Who thought on three men dead.

Wilfred Wilson Gibson

Puzzles

The most haunted house in England

In this passage some words have been left out. Read the story and try to work out what the words should be. Then write down the number of each blank and the word you think should go there.

Ghostly figures of headless coachmen and ....¹..... nun, an old-time coach drawn ....²..... two bay horses, which appears and ....³..... mysteriously, and dragging footsteps in empty ....⁴..... . All these ingredients of a first-class ....⁵..... story are awaiting investigation by psychic ....⁶..... near Long Melford, Suffolk.

The scene ....⁷..... the ghostly visitations is the Rectory ....⁸..... Borley, a few miles from Long ....⁹..... . It is a building erected on ....¹⁰.... part of the site of a ....¹¹.... monastery, which, in the Middle Ages, ...¹².... the scene of a gruesome tragedy. ....¹³.... present rector, the Rev G. E. Smith, ...¹⁴.... his wife made the Rectory their ....¹⁵.... in the face of warnings by ....¹⁶.... occupiers. Since their arrival they have ....¹⁷.... puzzled and startled by a series ....¹⁸.... peculiar happenings which cannot be explained, ...¹⁹.... which confirm the rumours which they heard ....²⁰..... moving in.

The first untoward happening ....²¹.... the sound of slow dragging footsteps ....²².... the floor of an unoccupied room. ....²³.... one night Mr Smith, armed with ....²⁴.... hockey stick, sat in the room ....²⁵.... waited for the noise. Once again ....²⁶.... came – the sound of feet in ....²⁷.... kind of slippers treading on the ....²⁸.... boards. Mr Smith lashed out with ....²⁹.... stick at the spot where the ....³⁰.... seemed to be, but the stick ....³¹.... through the empty air and the ....³².... continued across the room.

Then a ....³³.... girl brought from London, suddenly gave ....³⁴.... after two days' work, declaring emphatically ....³⁵.... she had seen a nun walking ....³⁶.... the wood at the back of ....³⁷.... house. Finally comes the remarkable story ....³⁸.... an old-fashioned coach seen twice on ....³⁹.... lawn by a servant, which remained ....⁴⁰.... sight long enough for the girl to ....⁴¹.... the brown colour of the ....⁴².... .

This same servant also declares that ....⁴³.... has seen a nun leaning over ....⁴⁴.... gate near the house. The villagers ....⁴⁵.... the neighbourhood of the Rectory after ....⁴⁶.... , and will not pass it. Peculiarly ....⁴⁷.... , all these 'visitations' coincide with the ....⁴⁸.... of a tragedy which, according to ....⁴⁹.... , occurred at the monastery which once ....⁵⁰.... on this spot.

Word study 1: Nouns into adjectives

Many nouns can be changed into adjectives by adding a suffix.

ghost + ly   ghostly

For each of the nouns in column 1, choose a suffix from column 2 that will turn it into an adjective.

1		2	
faith	gold	-ly	-ed
girl	lady	-al	-en
talent	coast	-ish	-ful
king		-like	

Word study 2: Ghostly words

Each of these words is concerned with the theme of this unit.

occult   astrology
spook   apparition
poltergeist   sorcerer
exorcise   medium

1 Write each one on a separate line.
2 Write the meanings of any that you know alongside the words.
3 Try to guess the others.
4 Look *all* the words up in a dictionary.
5 Write the correct meanings of any that you got wrong.

Word puzzle

Copy the puzzle and then complete it. If you fill in the answers to all the clues, you will find out the key word.

Clues
1 The name of the dead spaceman. (p. 139)
2 Mind-reading. (p. 134)
3 _____ at Grange Towers. (p. 136)
4 'We only saw a table, spread
   For dinner, meat and cheese and _____...' (p. 141)
5 Where 'we' saw Miss Wickerby. (p. 135)
6 What caused the *Titanic* to sink. (p. 134)
7 Laura's brother. (p. 132)

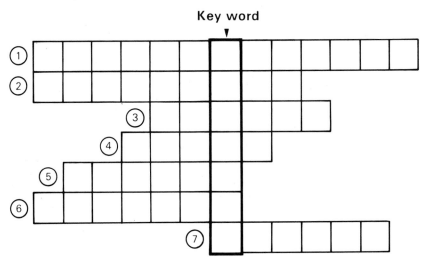

ESCAPE FROM KRAZNIR

How the story begins

There are two countries separated by a river: Kraznir and Slinsil.
The people of Kraznir are fierce and warlike. Their land is poor and
little will grow there. Their king is called Krill and lives in a castle in
the mountains. To the south of Kraznir is Slinsil. It is a rich and
beautiful country, whose people love peace.

  Rumours have reached Slinsil that Krill is planning to send an
army to attack them. They hurriedly prepare to defend themselves.
They send a team of spies to Kraznir to find out about Krill's plans.
They want to know when and where he intends to attack. The spies
are successful. Deep in the cellars of Castle Krill they find the
complete battle plan. This, and many other valuable documents, is
stored in a large wooden chest. Now the spies have got to get the
chest and all its contents safely back to Slinsil.

  You are the leader of the spies.

147

Your companions

You have four companions: a wizard, a hobbit, a warrior, and a dwarf.

Touchfire the Wizard

Touchfire can make himself invisible. He can turn evil creatures to stone, but this spell only lasts for five minutes and does not work near water.

Doughty the Warrior

Doughty wears strong armour and carries a huge sword. He is very brave and strong.

Littlejohn the Hobbit

Littlejohn is very small, only about a metre tall. He is quick and light-footed, but not very strong. He carries a small dagger. Because he is so nimble he can usually escape from danger, provided he is not too tired.

Athor the Dwarf

He, too, is short, but he is broad and strong. He is accustomed to living underground, so can see in the dark and can make himself almost invisible. He is very brave and carries a battle axe.

Instructions Read pages 146 and 147 very carefully. Make sure that you understand all the details about your four companions. Try to remember what each one can do – what is special about him. When you have done this, turn to pages 148 and 149 for the first part of the story.

Day one

The five of you have to escape from Castle Krill and begin the journey home to Slinsil. You need to do these three things:

1 Steal food for your journey home.
2 Work out the safest route out of the dungeons.
3 Escape with the chest and the food you have stolen.

Plan of the castle basement

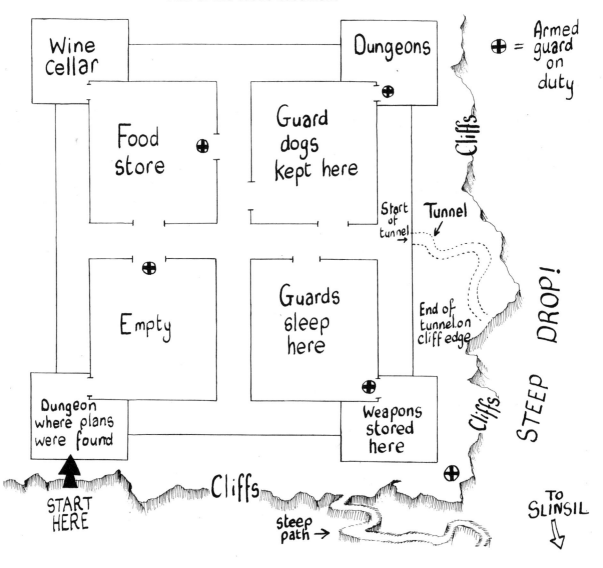

← Castle walls

The
end
of
the
tunnel

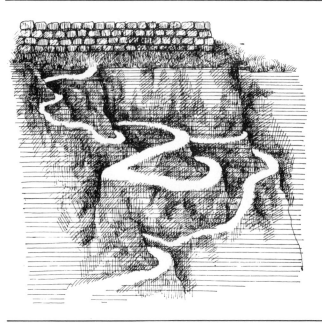

Castle walls

The
path
down
the
cliffs

Instructions   1   Study the map and the pictures carefully.
2   Decide how to get to the food without a general alarm being raised.
3   Decide how to get from the food store to the start of the tunnel without being stopped.
4   Decide how to get past the guard on the cliff top.
5   Decide how the chest and the food are going to be carried.

Writing   Write the story of how you and your companions escape.

Day two

You have escaped from the castle and are now high up in the mountains. It is very cold. You have spent the night on a narrow ledge. It is just getting light. There is a sheer drop below you and steep cliffs above. Suddenly you hear noises. They get louder.

It is the followers of Krill. He may have sent Spiders, *or* Wargs, *or* Orcs.

Giant Spiders

They are two metres across.
They have legs that are
3 metres long. Their bite is
poisonous to anyone, except
dwarves.

Wargs

Wargs are man-eating wolves,
who also enjoy a meal of
hobbit or dwarf. They are
twice as big as the biggest
dog you have ever seen. They
do not touch wizards, because
wizards throw fireballs at
them. Wargs are terrified of
any kind of fire.

Orcs

Orcs are vicious, mean
monsters which eat
absolutely any living creature.
They carry very sharp spears
and have cruel teeth, but they
wear no armour. Therefore
they can easily be injured – if
you can get close enough.

Instructions

1 Decide whether it is Spiders, Wargs, or Orcs that are attacking.
2 Decide how your party can defend themselves against them.
3 Decide whether anyone is likely to get injured.

Writing   Tell the story of what happens when the enemy attack.

Day three

At last you have left the mountains. Now you have reached the River Glin. Krill's soldiers are still following you and are not far behind you. You must cross the river quickly. It is very deep and fast-flowing, so you cannot swim it. Luckily you have found a small boat.

Information
1 The boat will carry only four people, or the same weight as four people.
2 It needs one person to row it and one person to steer it.
3 There are five of you.
4 There are also two bags of food. Each bag weighs the same as one person.
5 There is also the chest. It weighs the same as one person.
6 The wizard's magic does not work on this river.

Instructions
Work out the shortest number of trips in which you can ferry the whole party and its luggage across the river. Do not forget that each time you have to send two people back across the river – the boat cannot row and steer itself!

Writing
When you have worked out the answer, write it down.

Just as you start to put the plan into action, something terrible happens:

Instructions

1 Decide what is causing this.
2 Decide what happens to the boat.
3 Decide what the rest of you do about it.

Writing

Tell the story of what happens. Begin from when the boat starts on its first journey.

Day four

You have crossed the river and reached the stony desert. You are all very tired. You have not eaten for nearly six hours. It is beginning to get dark. You have decided to make camp in a rocky place.

Just at that moment there is a fearful noise. You look round and find yourselves face to face with a terrible creature. It is nearly dark and at first you cannot see whether it is a Dragon, or a Margatroth or a Balrog.

Dragon

The dragon is 15 metres long and, like most dragons, breathes flame. It can kill by burning or by crushing its enemies in its jaws. The wizard is sometimes able to speak to it and soothe its anger. This does not always work, so it is unwise to rely on it. The warrior can kill it with his sword – if he can get close enough.

Margatroth

The Margatroth is a huge creature with two heads, one at each end. It has fierce teeth and six legs. It is very dangerous to all living creatures, except hobbits. They are too small for the Margatroth to see easily. It can only be killed by chopping off one of its heads.

Balrog

The Balrog's body is made of fire. It can glow dully or flame brilliantly. The only weapon you can use against it is water. The only water you have is your small supply of drinking water, and you are in the middle of a desert. There is one chink of hope: the Balrog only moves quite slowly.

Instructions

1 Decide which of these creatures is attacking you.
2 Decide how you and your companions can defend yourselves against it.
3 Decide what happens in the end.

Writing Tell the story of what happens when the creature attacks.

Day five

At last you have reached the Forest of Haag. You have to find your way through this thick and dangerous forest. On the other side is the River Slin and freedom. The forest is the home of an evil magician, Nehemath. If anyone tries to pass through the forest he becomes very angry and tries to stop them. In addition, you have a number of problems:

1 You have lost all your food and are all becoming weaker.
2 The hobbit is now so weak that he has to be carried.
3 You may also have lost your water on day four (The Balrog).
4 The wizard's spells do not work in the forest itself.

Instructions
1 Decide what nasty scheme Nehemath has to stop you passing through the wood.
2 Decide how your party tries to survive.
3 Decide what happens in the end.

Writing
Tell the story of what happens. Include these points in your story:
1 Entering the wood and discovering what Nehemath is up to.
2 Trying to escape.
3 Escaping from the wood and crossing the River Slin.
4 Being welcomed to Slinsil.

Section B: Skills

Nouns and adjectives

Nouns Nouns are words we use to name:

people : man, professor
places : garage, hill
things : stone, telescope
ideas : peace, terror

In this passage, all the *nouns* have been printed in *italics*.

I opened the *door* very quietly and walked into the *room*. It was dark and quiet. My *eyes* got used to the *darkness* and I saw in the *corner* a large wooden *box*. I walked across and opened the *lid*. It was full of *diamonds* and other *jewels*. Just as I was looking at all these precious *stones*, the *door* opened. A *man* walked in, carrying a *gun*.

Adjectives We use adjectives to qualify nouns.
'Qualify' means 'say more about'.
In this passage all the **adjectives** are in **bold** type.

The gun looked very **large** and **dangerous**. I was **terrified**. I was so **frightened** I could not move. The jewels fell from my **nervous** grasp. The man jerked the gun towards a **green** door at the **far** end of the room. I walked slowly across to it. Then I stopped, **uncertain** what to do next.

Further example In this passage the *nouns* are in *italics*. All the **adjectives** are in **bold** type.

The *armourer's forge* was **east** of the *river*, in **that** *part* of the *city* **called** *Chesil*. It was a **large cavernous** *building*, its *floor* of **ancient** *stone* **cracked** in *places* but **all** of a *piece*; **dark** except where the **great central** *fire* sent *sparks* springing up towards the **square** *hole* in the **timbered** *roof*. In the *dimness* the *dwarfs* moved here and there to the *clang* of *metal* on *metal*.

John Christopher, *The Prince in Waiting*

Exercises

A   **Make a list of all the nouns in this passage.**

No one can tell you exactly who it was now, but it was quite certainly one of the youngest children that invented the name 'Trillions'. You can imagine a group of children squatting on the ground, scraping together heaps of brightly coloured, mysterious grit that had fallen from the sky . . .

   'I've got millions!'
   'I've got billions!'
   'I've got trillions!'

   Trillions it was from then on. The name fitted perfectly. It had the right hard, bright sound to it – and Trillions were hard and bright. It suggests millions upon millions – and the Trillions were everywhere, sprinkling roads and gardens and roofs and even the firesides of people's homes with a glittery dusting of tiny jewels.

Nicholas Fisk: *Trillions*

B   **Copy out this passage and fill in each of the blanks with a suitable noun.**

As I was walking along the _____ I suddenly saw a large _____ coming towards me. I was surprised because it was still dark and there were no _____ around. It was a cold _____ and I was wearing my _____ . As the _____ approached, I saw there were two more _____ behind. This frightened me and made me wish I was still in my _____ .

C   **Make a list of all the adjectives in this passage.**

His name was Squib. At least, that was what the little ones called him. 'There's Squib,' they shouted, racing across the shaved grass of the park to where he waited by the swings and the sandpit and the seesaw, a small, pale child.

   'Squib's not a name,' the bigger ones said, and once, in the beginning, Robin had asked him, 'What's your real name?' but he hung his head and said nothing as he usually did when an older child or an adult spoke to him, so Squib he became.

Nina Bawden: *Squib*

Verbs and adverbs

Verbs
Verbs are words we use to describe **actions** : run, hit
states   : seem, appear
changes : become, grow

In this passage all the *verbs* are in *italics*.

Henderson *runs* down the right wing . . . He *dodges* beautifully past James . . . He *passes* to Bradley . . . Bradley *puts* it inside to Wood . . . He *goes* round Mason . . . He *shoots* . . . GOAL!

There is also a group of verbs called auxiliaries which go together with other verbs:

be am is are was were being been
has have had having
may might can could must ought
will would shall should do did

In this passage all the *verbs* (including *auxiliaries*) are in *italics*.

Friday *was* a bad day. Things *began to go* wrong as soon as I *woke* up. I *got* out of bed and *put* my foot right in a cup of tea my mother *had left* for me. Then, as I *was brushing* my teeth, the toothbrush *snapped* in half and I *cut* my lip. Even then things *would* not *have been* too bad, if I *had* not *tripped* on the top stair as I *was going* down to breakfast. I *am writing* this from hospital.

Adverbs
Adverbs modify verbs, adjectives, or other adverbs.
'Modify' means 'say more about'.

In this paragraph the **adverbs** are in **bold** type.

Jason peered **guiltily** round the door. He was feeling **very** unhappy because he had **just** broken his father's new camera. He had seen it on the table, **just** lying **there**. He had picked it up **excitedly**, pretended to take a couple of action photographs, and **somehow** he had dropped it. He had picked it up **extremely carefully** but he knew **immediately** it was broken.

Exercises

A   Make a list of all the verbs in this passage.

At last Peterson saw the elephant. He raised his rifle slowly. He aimed it carefully and held it very steady. Then the elephant moved: it turned and walked slowly away. Peterson lowered the rifle again. He settled down beside the tree and waited for another chance.

B   Make a list of all the verbs in this passage. Make sure each time that you write out the whole verb (including auxiliaries).

Two old women were gossiping over their garden fence.

'You know Mrs Turner, used to live at number nineteen, and went to America with that flyer?'

'I know her well,' said the other.

'Well,' said the first, 'I hear she's dead.'

'Don't you believe it,' said her friend. 'I've heard nothing, and if it was true she would have told me herself, for she writes to me about everything.'

Aidan Chambers, *Funny Folk*

C   Make a list of all the adverbs in this passage.

He ran quickly down the street. He looked anxiously left and right. Fortunately everything was quiet. He felt tired and rather unhappy to be running away so soon. He reached the crossroads and stopped. He started again and turned into the High Street. Suddenly he stopped. There was the sound of footsteps behind him. His heart beat violently. He was being followed!

D   Complete each of these sentences by filling in the blanks with suitable adverbs. Only write one word for each blank.

1   Mary dances _____ but Hilda can only sing _____ .
2   He ran _____ down the street and collided with a policeman who was standing _____ on the pavement.
3   The elephant moved _____ towards the hunter who was trembling _____ .
4   George plays football _____ .
5   I have never seen John behave so _____ .

Sentences

Types of sentence

There are three types of sentence:

Statement : Mike went home from school.
Question : Who has gone home?
Command : Go home at once!

Subject

Every sentence has a subject:

Subject	Rest of the sentence
Mike *Who*	went home from school. has gone home?

In commands the subject is *you*. It is usually left out.

(*you*)　　　　Go home at once!

Verb

Every sentence has a verb:

Subject	Verb	Rest of the sentence
Mike *Who* (*you*)	**went** **has gone** **Go**	home from school. home from school? home at once!

Some more examples

In each example the *subject* is in *italics*. The **verb** is in **bold** type.

Statements:　*Mary's pet guinea pig* **is called** Montezuma.
　　　　　　　Last Monday night *Elton* **broke** his arm.
　　　　　　　Pink elephants **are** seldom **seen** in Lewisham.

Questions:　Where on earth **have** *you* **been**?
　　　　　　　Did *Winifred* really **go** to Antarctica last summer?
　　　　　　　Who **is** that strange man over there?

Commands:　**Get** off my foot at once!
　　　　　　　Help!

Exercises

A **Write down whether each of these sentences is a statement, a question, or a command.**

1 Are you sure that Dave has bought a giraffe?
2 Stop it at once!
3 You really do believe in ghosts, do you?
4 Jane, leave that switch alone.
5 In the match, Suzanne scored three rounders.
6 If you don't get off my foot, I shall scream!
7 What is zircon?
8 Please do as you are told.
9 I'm afraid I haven't a clue.
10 Get out your exercise books.

B **Write down the subject of each of the sentences in Exercise A.**

C **Write down the verb of each of the sentences in Exercise A.**

D **Write out these sentences and fill the gaps with suitable verbs.**

1 Last weekend Janet _____ all the way to Blackpool.
2 On the way she _____ her purse.
3 So she _____ the police station.
4 The sergeant _____ very helpful.
5 He _____ her not to worry.
6 After that Janet _____ to her aunt's house in Blackpool.
7 There she _____ a huge tea.
8 That evening the telephone _____ .
9 It _____ the police sergeant.
10 Someone _____ Janet's purse.

E **Use this table to make up ten correct sentences that make sense.**

Subject	Verb	Rest of the Sentence
All my friends	is	angry with me.
Our Alsation dog	visited	the ball away.
It	wanted to know	hardworking pupils.
A ghost hunter	admire	dark.
My parents	has been playing	the old manor house.
David	is made	your name.
Teachers	behaves	of wood.
This desk	are	that?
Whoever	kicked	badly at school.
Desdemona	said	with a bone.

Note: you can use any of these parts in more than one sentence.

Agreement

Singular and plural

Singular means one.
Plural means more than one.

The subject of a sentence can be singular or plural.

Sentences with *singular* subjects:

Peter Ericson is a famous explorer.
Pride goes before a fall.
My Aunt Jemima's favourite pet dog bit her.

Sentences with *plural* subjects:

50,000 Liverpool fans saw their team win the cup.
Julie and Hilary are sisters.
They go to the pictures every Saturday.

The verb

In a sentence the verb must *agree* with the subject.
Singular subject : **singular verb**.

Peter Ericson **is** a famous explorer. *He* **likes** to travel around the world to remote places. *He* **takes** lots of equipment with him when *he* **goes**.

I often **go** to the shops after school. *I* **like** to buy ice cream. Sometimes *I* **buy** sweets which *I* **take** to school next day to share with my friends. Sometimes *I* **am** greedy and **eat** them all myself.

Plural subject : **plural verb.**

Julie and Hilary **are** sisters. *They* **don't like** going out together. *They* **prefer** to have separate friends. Sometimes, *they* both **take** their friends home to listen to records.

We **like** to go to the pictures on Saturday. Sometimes *we* **take** our boyfriends with us if the film is one *we* all **want** to see. Sometimes *they* **choose** to go to the football match.

Exercises

A **Write down the subject of each of these sentences. Say whether it is singular or plural.**

1 Where is your father's hammer?
2 All my friends like skating.
3 My sister and I share everything.
4 The boiling point of water is 100 degrees Centigrade.
5 Science and Geography are Dave's favourite subjects.
6 The teachers at our school are usually quite friendly.
7 Trees can be deciduous or evergreen.
8 Oaks, beeches and elms are deciduous.
9 Is our class being kept in tonight?
10 Who did that?

B **Write out each of these sentences, adding a suitable subject.**

1 _____ is no superman.
2 _____ are usually very good at swimming.
3 _____ was a silly thing to do.
4 _____ were the only ones left in the room.
5 _____ want to go to Scotland in the summer.
6 _____ wants to become a professional photographer.
7 _____ is walking along the street at this very moment.
8 _____ were living next door to us for two years.
9 At this time of year _____ like to go swimming in the sea.
10 Very unexpectedly _____ came home early.

C **For each of these sentences, choose the correct word in brackets to fit the space.**

1 The chief of the detectives _____ (wishes/wish) to speak to you.
2 Jimmie, Mike, Pete, and you all _____ (plays/play) the fool in English lessons.
3 Paper and wood _____ (starts/start) a fire well.
4 Either paper or wood _____ (starts/start) a fire well.
5 As leader of the gang, I _____ (are/am/is) the one who _____ (gives/give) the orders.
6 Mr and Mrs Brown, their son Peter, and their daughter Sue _____ (was/were) driving into town yesterday.
7 The clock on the church is always right and the clock on the school _____ (is/am/are) always wrong.
8 My brother and I _____ (is/am/are) the best of friends.
9 The cleverest of my friends _____ (is/are) Hilary.
10 There _____ (is/are) three different snakes in this country but only one of them _____ (is/are) poisonous.

Sentences, capital letters, and full stops

Sentences Every sentence must be separated from other sentences. This is done by punctuation.

Begin every sentence with a capital letter and end it with a full stop.

Capital letters Capital letters are also used for these things:

1	The word 'I':	I
2	Names:	James Witherspoon
		Coca Cola
3	The main words in titles:	Watership Down
		Minister of Education
4	For days and months:	Monday
		December
5	For initials:	J. J. Witherspoon
		BBC

Full stops Full stops are also used for these things:

1	After initials:	J. J. Witherspoon
2	After some abbreviations:	Sun. for Sunday
		Oct. for October
		Yorks. for Yorkshire

Exceptions These are often written without a full stop:
1 The initials of very well known organisations:
   BBC UNESCO FBA
2 These titles: Mr Mrs Ms Dr Revd Mme Mlle

Exercises

A **Write this paragraph out as separate sentences. Use full stops and capital letters.**

when the children reached the farm they found that there was no one around a large black dog barked at them angrily some chickens clucked at them apart from this they could see and hear nothing they tried the door it was open nervously david went inside.

B **Write this paragraph out putting in full stops and capital letters where necessary.**

last week strange things began to happen at giggleswick peculiar noises were heard and the earth trembled several times after this things became peaceful again and people thought little of it then last night it happened just after dark the sky was lit up with coloured lights a white saucer-shaped spaceship descended slowly onto the playing field and came slowly to rest for a while nothing happened at last a door opened in the side of the ship by now a crowd had gathered on the field everyone watched in excitement they wondered who or what would come out of the door the creature who finally came out looked just like a human being in fact it was a human being it was a tall man with dark hair he was holding a large book he went up to the mayor of giggleswick who was standing with the crowd he said, 'mr mayor, this is your life.'

C **Write out these sentences, putting in full stops and capital letters where necessary.**

1 peter harman works for the bbc
2 last summer my family went by british rail to blackpool
3 during bad weather the aa and the rac help stranded motorists
4 helen's birthday is in may but mary's is in august
5 i enjoy watching tv and i prefer itv to bbc
6 my favourite subjects at school are english and pe
7 last christmas i was given a kodak camera and a scalextric set

D **Write down the abbreviated forms of the following.**

1 North Atlantic Treaty Organisation
2 United Nations Educational Scientific and Cultural Organisation
3 National Health Service
4 Bachelor of Science
5 On Her Majesty's Service
6 for example
7 centimetre
8 miles per hour

Commas

1 Commas are used to separate the different things in a list.

My interests are walking, road running, reading and swimming.

2 Commas are used to mark off the first part of the sentence and separate it from the rest.

When the children had finished eating, the headmaster made an announcement.

3 Commas are used to mark off the middle part of a sentence and separate it from the rest.

I saw Peter James, the boy you kicked, in the street.

4 Commas are used to mark off the last part of a sentence and separate it from the rest.

John is coming with us tomorrow, I hope.

5 Commas are used in direct speech. (page 174)

Further example: In this passage the commas make the story much easier to understand.

One morning a large wooden case was brought to the farmhouse, and Bevis, impatient to see what was in it, ran for the hard chisel and the hammer, and would not consent to put off the work of undoing it for a moment. It must be done directly. The case was very broad and nearly square, but only a few inches deep, and was formed of thin boards. They placed it for him upon the floor, and, kneeling down, he tapped the chisel, driving the edge in under the lid, and so starting the nails. Twice he hit his fingers in his haste, once so hard that he dropped the hammer, but he picked it up again and went on as before, till he had loosened the lid all round.

Richard Jefferies, *Bevis*

Exercises

A **Write out these sentences, adding commas where they are needed.**

1 My favourite foods are smoky bacon crisps vanilla ice cream fish and chips and chocolate.
2 Our family went to Birmingham on Monday to North Wales on Tuesday and to Anglesey on Wednesday.
3 Mary has nearly a whole shelf of toy animals and she only wants a chimpanzee to fill it up.
4 When the clock struck my mother said it was time to go to school.
5 My uncle Charlie who lives near Newcastle has two greyhounds.
6 When I lived in Germany for a year I managed to make myself understood even though I speak little German.
7 Before Pete left Dave lost his temper.
8 The main towns of Hertfordshire are St Albans Hertford Watford Hatfield and Hemel Hempstead.
9 Michael Grey my best friend has just broken his leg.
10 When the rope snapped the climber fell a hundred feet.

B **Write out this paragraph, adding capital letters, full stops and commas where needed.**

when i was in paris last month i saw eden witherspoon the young pop star he was jogging along the champs elysees i rushed up to him and asked him for his autograph unfortunately i had forgotten my pen so he could not sign still it was very exciting to see such a famous person after that we went up the eiffel tower and took a trip along the river seine in a glass-topped boat the boat was very crowded so it was quite difficult to see but i was still able to enjoy the trip i shall never forget my holiday in paris.

C **Write out this paragraph putting in necessary punctuation.**

more than eleven hours of incessant hard travelling brought us early in the morning to the end of a range of mountains in front of us there lay a piece of low broken desert land which we must now cross the sun was not long up and shone straight in our eyes a little thin mist went up from the face of the moorland like smoke so that there might have been twenty squadron of dragoons there and we none the wiser.

Apostrophes

Omission Apostrophes are used to show where one or more letters have been omitted, or missed out, for example:

we have	becomes	**we've**
who is	becomes	**who's**
are not	becomes	**aren't**
they are	becomes	**they're**
Dad will	becomes	**Dad'll**
you are	becomes	**you're**
I would	becomes	**I'd**
she might have	becomes	**she might've**

Possession Apostrophes are used to show possession – to show that something belongs to someone.

1 We add **'s** to words that do not end in s.
> **Jane's** bike   **Gran's** house
> the **man's** foot   **people's** problems

2 We add just **'** to words that do end in s.
> the **girls'** mother   **Charles'** idea
> **James'** friend   **animals'** homes

Exceptions its (meaning belonging to it)
his
hers
yours
ours
theirs

171

Exercises

A   **Write the following in their short form, using apostrophes where necessary.**
1   they would
2   I have
3   we shall
4   I am not
5   you would not have
6   he did not
7   she may not
8   you are
9   it is
10   we might have

B   **Write out this paragraph, putting in apostrophes where needed.**

Ive got three requests for this next number. Its a track from the new album by the Grotts. The Grottsve just got back from that great American tour of theirs andve followed up the success of 'Its all hers' with a single called 'You shouldve told me.' This ones been requested by Dave Plinge of Beckenham. Dave says hed like me to play it for all his mates at St James School, Beckenham.

C   **Write out these sentences putting in the correct form of the words in brackets.**

1   My friend, (who's/whose) bike I borrowed, wants it back.
2   (It's/Its) not raining today.
3   Those books the boys lost were not (there's/theirs/their's).
4   Our dog has got a thorn in (it's/its) paw.
5   I say that the money is (your's/yours) but Sue says (it's/its) (her's/hers).
6   (Theirs/There's/Theres) a wasp on your neck.
7   We (havent/have'nt/haven't) seen each other for days.
8   (Theyve/Theyv'e/They've) just gone home.
9   You (werent/weren't/were'nt) home when I called.
10   I thought the bike belonged to (James/Jame's/James') but he said it was (Francis'/Francis) machine.

D   **Write out this paragraph putting in all the necessary punctuation.**

i forgot to tell you in my last letter that ive been chosen to swim for the county its a great honour and mums very excited she says all the familyll come to see me swim even gran if shes well itll be exciting all right im only hoping i dont let everyone down ive been training every day at the baths and im feeling very fit the matchs on saturday week so think of me then

Script

Script is the way in which conversations are written down in plays.

1 The names of the speakers are written in capital letters.
The names are put underneath each other.

2 A colon (:) is put after the name of each speaker.

3 Only the words they actually say are written.
Each new line of speech starts underneath the one before.

As a script the conversation looks like this:

ANNE: Look! There's a cave.

MIKE: Let's go and explore!

ANNE: All right.

MIKE: Come on. Are you scared?

ANNE: Of course not.

Stage directions If you want to, you can add a description of what the people do and how they speak. These explanations are written between brackets and underlined:

ANNE: (Pointing at the cliffs.) Look! There's a cave.

MIKE: Let's go and explore!

ANNE: All right.

(They walk towards the cliffs.)

MIKE: (Going into the cave.) Come on. Are you scared?

ANNE: (Frightened.) Of course not.

Exercises

A Write this conversation as a script. Give the two boys names.

B Write the script again. This time put in all the necessary stage directions.

C On page 90 there is a conversation between Theseus and Skiron. Write it as a script, adding stage directions where necessary.

Direct speech

Direct speech is the way in which conversations are written down in stories.

1   The words spoken are always put in inverted commas:

single   '_____'

or double   "_____"

2   Each new piece of speech begins with a capital letter.

3   Each piece of speech ends with one of these:

,   .   ?   or   !

4   If you put the *he said* words before the speech, put a comma before the inverted commas:

He said, '_____.'

5   If you put the *he said* words in the middle of a piece of speech, you need not start the second part with a capital letter, unless the word needs one anyway.

6   Every time there is a new speaker, start a new line.

In direct speech the conversation looks like this:

'Look! There's a cave,' said Anne.
'Let's go and explore,' Mike suggested.
'All right.'
They went towards the cave. When they got there, Anne did not seem very keen to go in.
'Come on,' said Mike. 'Are you scared?'
'Of course not,' she answered.

Exercises **A** **Tell this story, putting the conversation into direct speech.**

B **Write this conversation in direct speech.**

MOTHER: What were you doing in town this morning?

SHEILA: (Nervously.) I wasn't in town.

MOTHER: Yes you were. I saw you.

SHEILA: (Guiltily.) I wasn't Mum. Honest.

MOTHER: (Beginning to get angry.) Sheila!

SHEILA: (Looking away and fidgeting.) Oh . . . well . . .

MOTHER: You were supposed to be in school. How come you were in town?

SHEILA: (Embarrassed.) I suppose I'd better tell you.

MOTHER: I think you had.

C **Write the rest of Sheila's conversation with her mother, in which she explains why she was in town and what she was doing.**

Addresses and envelopes

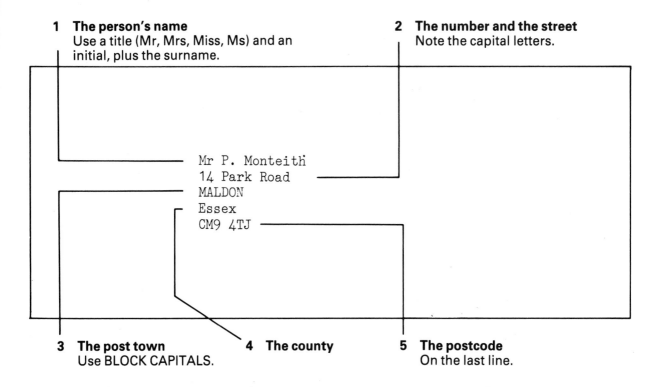

1 The person's name
Use a title (Mr, Mrs, Miss, Ms) and an initial, plus the surname.

2 The number and the street
Note the capital letters.

```
Mr P. Monteith
14 Park Road
MALDON
Essex
CM9 4TJ
```

3 The post town
Use BLOCK CAPITALS.

4 The county

5 The postcode
On the last line.

Spacing Always try to leave plenty of space on the envelope all round the address. Always make sure that there is room for:

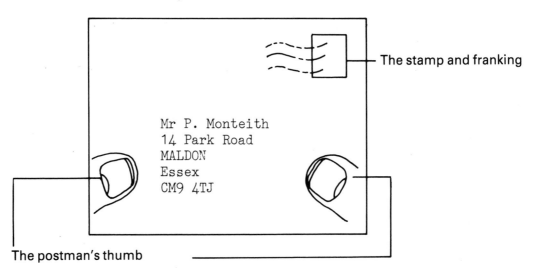

The stamp and franking

```
Mr P. Monteith
14 Park Road
MALDON
Essex
CM9 4TJ
```

The postman's thumb

Exercises

A Draw a rectangle about 15 cm x 10 cm. Use it as an 'envelope' and address it to yourself.

B Draw an 'envelope' about 15 cm x 10 cm. Address it to your headteacher at your school.

C Find out the full addresses of the following:

1 Your local greengrocer's shop
2 Your local electricity showroom
3 Your local council office
4 Your doctor
5 Someone in your class
6 One of your relations

D Choose two of the addresses in exercise C and write 'envelopes' to them.

E Find out the full names and addresses of as many of these people as you can:

1 The Queen
2 The President of the United States of America
3 The Prime Minister
4 BBC tv
5 Your local football club

F Choose two of the names in exercise E and address 'envelopes' to them.

G Some county names do not have to be written in full in addresses. Write the full name of the following abbreviated counties.

1 Lincs.
2 N. Yorks.
3 Berks.
4 Wilts.
5 Leics.
6 Staffs.
7 Lancs.
8 Herts.

Letters

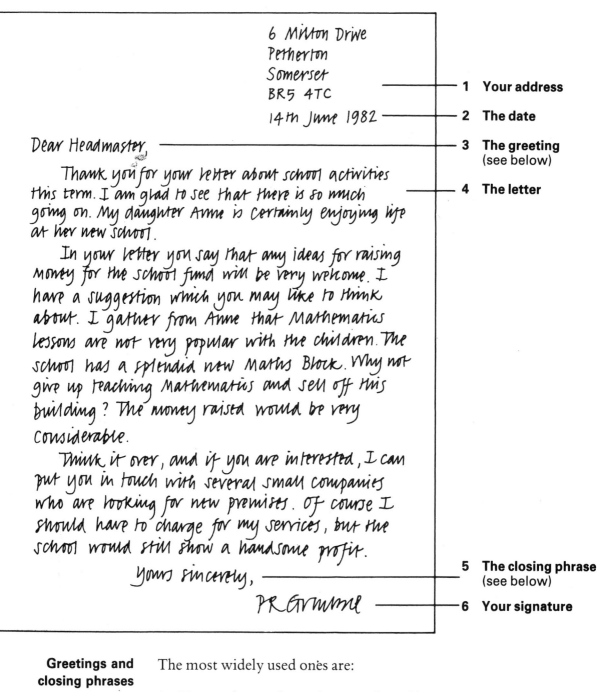

6 Milton Drive
Petherton
Somerset
BR5 4TC — **1** **Your address**

14th June 1982 — **2** **The date**

Dear Headmaster, — **3** **The greeting**
(see below)

　　Thank you for your letter about school activities
this term. I am glad to see that there is so much
going on. My daughter Anne is certainly enjoying life
at her new school. — **4** **The letter**

　　In your letter you say that any ideas for raising
money for the school fund will be very welcome. I
have a suggestion which you may like to think
about. I gather from Anne that Mathematics
lessons are not very popular with the children. The
school has a splendid new Maths Block. Why not
give up teaching Mathematics and sell off this
building? The money raised would be very
considerable.

　　Think it over, and if you are interested, I can
put you in touch with several small companies
who are looking for new premises. Of course I
should have to charge for my services, but the
school would still show a handsome profit.

　　　　Yours sincerely, — **5** **The closing phrase**
(see below)

　　　　　PR Grimble — **6** **Your signature**

Greetings and closing phrases

The most widely used ones are:

1　To people you do not know at all: Dear Sir,
　　　Yours faithfully,

2　To people you know a little: Dear Mr/Mrs/Miss/Ms _____,
　　　Yours sincerely,

Exercises

A   The letter on the opposite page has been written to the headmaster of a school just like yours. Write his reply.

B   Write a letter in reply to this advertisement:

The JUNIOR RANGERS CLUB is an organization which provides holidays for young people from all over Britain. JUNIOR RANGERS holidays are exciting – different – fun! If you go on a JR holiday you will meet people of your own age from all over the country. You will take part in all sorts of exciting activities. If you would like to join JUNIOR RANGERS, write *now* to:

    Mr P. Harris
    Junior Rangers Club
    15 Winterstoke Street
    HERTFORD
    SG17 9AY

Give your age and interests, and tell us the kind of thing you would like to do on an adventure holiday.

C   Your father has received the following letter. Write his answer to it.

                                    Seaview
                                    The Esplanade
                                    Eastbourne
                                    Sussex
                                    BR5 9BG

                                    17th September 1982

Dear Mr. Grey,

        Your family recently stayed at this guest house and occupied two rooms on the first floor.
        When I was clearing up after you had gone, I found a number of items in the room that your two sons had shared.
They were: 2 footballs
              1 football boot
              a road sign
              a fire extinguisher
              2 lengths of dry seaweed
              a full-size cardboard model of a donkey
              736 seashells

        I am sure that your sons would like to have their property back. I should certainly like to get rid of it. It is too much to send by post. I should be grateful if you would tell me how you propose to deal with the problem: will you come and collect the items or shall I throw them away? (The council have said that they will make a charge of £10 for collecting them - you would have to pay this.)
        I look forward to hearing from you.

        Yours sincerely,

        A Macphee

        A. Macphee

The dictionary: finding the word

fan belt, belt driving rotating fan. **fanlight,** semi-circular window over door.

fan² *n.* enthusiast, devotee. **fan mail,** letters from fans.

fanatic (fă-**nat**-ik) *n. & adj.* (person) filled with excessive or mistaken enthusiasm, esp. in religion. **fanatical** *adj.* **fanaticism** (fă-**nat**-i-sizm) *n.*

fanciful *adj.* imaginary; whimsical; quaint.

fancy *n.* (power of creating) mental image; something imagined; whim; fondness, liking. *adj.* ornamental, not plain; whimsical, extravagant. *v.t.* imagine; think, suppose; like. **fancy dress,** unusual costume, usu. representing fictitious or historical character.

fanfare *n.* flourish of trumpets.

fang *n.* canine tooth, esp. of dog or wolf; serpent's venom-tooth.

fantasia (fan-**tay**-zi-ă) *n.* (Mus.) composition in which form is subordinate to fancy; composition based on several familiar tunes.

fantastic *adj.* absurdly fanciful; odd, grotesque; (*informal*) excellent. **fantastically** *adv.*

fantasy *n.* imagination; fancy; fantastic idea or design.

far *adv.* (*farther, farthest, further, furthest*), at or to a great distance; by much. *adj.* distant. **faraway,** remote; dreamy. **far-fetched,** forced, unnatural. **far-flung,** widely extended. **far-sighted,** having foresight.

farad (**fa**-rad) *n.* (Electr.) unit of capacitance.

farce *n.* light dramatic work intended only to

fascinate *v.t.* make (victim) powerless by one's presence or look; charm irresistibly. **fascination** *n.*

Fascism (**fash**-izm) *n.* principles and organization of Italian nationalist anti-Communist dictatorship (1922–43); imitations of this in other countries. **fascist** *n. & adj.*

fashion *n.* shape, style; way, manner; prevailing style or custom, esp. in dress. *v.t.* form, shape. **fashionable** *adj.* of or in (latest) fashion.

fast¹ *v.i.* go without food, esp. as religious observance. *n.* going without food; day, season, of fasting.

fast² *adj.* quick, rapid; (of clock or watch) showing time ahead of the correct time; firmly attached; steadfast; (of colour) not fading, etc.; (of person) pleasure-seeking. *adv.* quickly; firmly, tightly.

fasten *v.* attach, fix; secure by tie or bond; become fast or secure. **fastener, fastening** *nn.*

fastidious (fas-**tid**-i-ŭs) *adj.* not easily pleased; careful in choosing; squeamish.

fastness *n.* (esp.) stronghold.

fat *adj.* (*fatter, fattest*), plump; having much fat; greasy, oily; fertile, abundant. *n.* oily substance in animal bodies; oily substance obtained from seeds, etc. **fat-head,** (*informal*) stupid person.

fatal *adj.* causing, ending in, death or disaster. **fatally** *adv.*

fatalism *n.* belief that all events are predetermined; submission to all that happens as inevitable. **fatalist** *n.* **fatalistic** *adj.*

The Oxford School Dictionary, 1981 edition

The words in a dictionary are in alphabetical order, of first letter:

         fast

         get

         high

If the first letters are the same, then look at the second letter:

         f**a**st

         f**e**tch

         f**i**t

and so on:

         fas**h**ion

         fas**t**

         fast**e**n

At the top of each page are printed the first and last words on that page.

The example above shows that these words are on page 110:
fantastic   farmer   fault

Exercises

A   **Write out each of these groups of words in alphabetical order.**

1   satchel   rabbit   quite   under   people   table   vase   open

2   ankle   habit   date   friend   white   extra   brand   catch

3   hoot   goat   hate   hump   grand   gate   heal   guzzle

4   out   prank   pinch   over   paddle   oasis   otherwise   pump   people   outside

5   gladiator   glossy   girth   glad   globular   glitter   given   glory   glisten   glade

B   **1**   **This is the heading of a dictionary page:**

mason   188   mattock

Which of these words go on that page:
massacre   mash   mask   matrix   mast   mattress   maul   mat

2   **Which of the following words go on this page:**

seal   277   secret

sear   sea   secret   secede   secretary   scuttle   search

3   **These are four pages in a dictionary:**

refuse	258	relative
relax	259	remunerate
Renaissance	260	reproach
reprobate	261	resolve

On which page will each of these words appear?
request   rely   repair   rent   regard   reside   remorse   reign

C   **Look up each of these groups of words in your dictionary. Write each word down and beside it write the number of the page it is on.**

1   splendid   soup   handy   prate   zebra   quaint   ranch   sprint

2   xylophone   topiary   remonstrate   impersonate   exaggerate   implicate   congratulate

3   national   reminiscence   antipodes   morgue   postscript   orderly   welter   denounce

The dictionary: getting the right meaning

fan belt, belt driving rotating fan. **fanlight,** semi-circular window over door.

fan² *n.* enthusiast, devotee. **fan mail,** letters from fans.

fanatic (fă-**nat**-ik) *n. & adj.* (person) filled with excessive or mistaken enthusiasm, esp. in religion. **fanatical** *adj.* **fanaticism** (fă-**nat**-i-sizm) *n.*

fanciful *adj.* imaginary; whimsical; quaint.

fancy *n.* (power of creating) mental image; something imagined; whim; fondness, liking. *adj.* ornamental, not plain; whimsical, extravagant. *v.t.* imagine; think, suppose; like. **fancy dress,** unusual costume, usu. representing fictitious or historical character.

fanfare *n.* flourish of trumpets.

fang *n.* canine tooth, esp. of dog or wolf; serpent's venom-tooth.

fantasia (fan-**tay**-zi-ă) *n.* (Mus.) composition in which form is subordinate to fancy; composition based on several familiar tunes.

fantastic *adj.* absurdly fanciful; odd, grotesque; (*informal*) excellent. **fantastically** *adv.*

fascinate *v.t.* make (victim) powerless by one's presence or look; charm irresistibly. **fascination** *n.*

Fascism (**fash**-izm) *n.* principles and organization of Italian nationalist anti-Communist dictatorship (1922-43); imitations of this in other countries. **fascist** *n. & adj.*

fashion *n.* shape, style; way, manner; prevailing style or custom, esp. in dress. *v.t.* form, shape. **fashionable** *adj.* of or in (latest) fashion.

fast¹ *v.i.* go without food, esp. as religious observance. *n.* going without food; day, season, of fasting.

fast² *adj.* quick, rapid; (of clock or watch) showing time ahead of the correct time; firmly attached; steadfast; (of colour) not fading, etc.; (of person) pleasure-seeking. *adv.* quickly; firmly, tightly.

fasten *v.* attach, fix; secure by tie or bond; become fast or secure. **fastener, fastening** *nn.*

fastidious (fas-**tid**-i-ŭs) *adj.* not easily pleased; careful in choosing; squeamish.

fastness *n.* (esp.) stronghold.

The Oxford School Dictionary, 1981 edition

The same word can have two completely different meanings.

fast¹ is completely different from **fast**²

fast¹: The prisoner fasted for fifteen days.
                 For Christians, Lent is a time of fast.

fast²: I caught the fast train.
                 Peter ran very fast.

Many words have a number of meanings that are different from each other, but not so different that they are given a different number.

fasten: The man fastened his raincoat.
               The crab fastened onto my finger.

When you look up a word, make sure that you find the right meaning.

1   Look for numbers against the word. If there are numbers, make sure you look at all the explanations.

2   Read all the explanations of the word.

3   Look at the sentence the word is in. Choose the explanation that fits the sentence best.

Exercises

A **Look up the words in bold type. Write down the dictionary explanation that fits the word as it is used in the sentence.**

1 The shopkeeper always likes to **bank** his money on Friday afternoon.
2 The badge that Philip has is an exact **match** for mine.
3 Inside the **hide** the birdwatcher kept his notebooks and binoculars.
4 There was a lot of **mould** on top of the jam, so we threw it away.
5 He had a large **tear** in his coat.
6 I like to **prune** my roses in November.
7 My foot has a small **corn** on it.
8 A soldier must always stay at his **post** during an attack.
9 The car was in the wrong **lane** to turn right.
10 I couldn't hear what she was saying as the **line** was not very clear.

B **The words in bold type have several different meanings. For each sentence write down the correct dictionary meaning of the word in bold type is, as it is used in the sentence.**

1 Her writing is always very **neat**.
2 The sailors drank their rum **neat**.
3 My father was very **cross** with me.
4 Our dog is a **cross** between a poodle and an alsation.
5 The judge went into **court**.
6 The tennis players were on **court** for three hours.
7 He is **proof** against any attack.
8 You cannot have any **proof** I did it.
9 Helen's hair is **fair**.
10 The punishment was not **fair**.

C **Find out the meanings of these words. Write a sentence containing each word and using it correctly.**

1	extension	6	forbear
2	schooner	7	rancour
3	facade	8	zither
4	diagnose	9	meagre
5	devout	10	browse

Spelling: rules

Long and short vowels
vowels: a e i o u
consonants: b c d f g h j k l m n p q r s t v w x
y z

LONG: *ta*pe   rec*e*de   gl*i*de   h*o*pe   f*u*me
SHORT: *ta*p   b*e*g   gr*i*t   h*o*p   sh*u*t

Adding **-ing** and **-ed**

tap*e* + ing = taping   tape → taping → taped
reced*e* + ing = receding   recede → receding → receded

tap + p + ing = tapping   tap → tapping → tapped
beg + g + ing = begging   beg → begging → begged

ie/ei
Rule: 'i before e except after c when the sound is long ee'
ie   **ei**
brief   ceiling
field   receive
believe   conceited

Exceptions: seize weird counterfeit neither

-ly
We add -ly to adjectives to make them into adverbs.

a   Most words do not have to change. You simply add -ly.
    sad → sadly
    great → greatly

b   If the word ends with -l, you still just add -ly.
    hopeful → hopefully
    loyal → loyally

c   If the word ends with -ll, just add -y
    dull → dully
    full → fully

d   If the word ends with -y, change the -y to -i and then add -ly.
    happy → happily   steady → steadily

Words that end in -y

a If we want to add anything to the end of a word that ends in -y, the spelling usually changes. -y becomes -i-:

cry	cries
spy	spies

b This does not happen if you add -ing:

cry	crying
spy	spying

c It does not happen if the letter before the -y is a vowel:

play	plays
pray	prays
boy	boys

Examples

happy	happier	happily	
funny	funnier	funnily	
cry	cries	cried	crying
spy	spies	spied	spying
play	plays	played	playing

Plurals Plural means 'more than one'. Most words follow these rules.

a Normally just add -s:

table	tables
chicken	chickens

b Words that end in -s: add -es:

boss	bosses
genius	geniuses

c Words that end in -ch: add -es:

crunch	crunches
church	churches

d Words that end in -f: change the -f to -ve:

half	halves
knife	knives

e Words that end in -y: see rule above.

Spelling: difficult words

here	Mary is here.	
hear	I can hear Mary coming.	

new	Do you like my new bike?
knew	I knew you would like it.

now	I want you to do it now.
know	I don't know what you mean.

loose	My tooth is loose.
lose	I don't want to lose another tooth.

there	Peter is over there.
their	The twins have lost their hats again.
they're	I think they're coming this way.

to	I'm going to London tomorrow.
two	I shall take two friends with me.
too	Dave is going, too.

weather	I hope the weather will be good.
whether	I don't know whether it will rain or not.

where	Where are you going?
were	They were both late for school.

who's	Do you know who's going to teach us English?
whose	Do you know whose book this is?

right	She doesn't know her right from her left.
write	I'll write you a letter as soon as I get there.

you're	They say you're only young once.
your	Give me your exercise book.

great	I think your party will be a great success.
grate	Please would you grate the cheese, Louise?

whole	During the afternoon we ate a whole bag of toffees.
hole	The money must have fallen through the hole in your pocket.

peace	The demonstrator carried a banner which read 'We want peace, not war'.
piece	The coded message was written on a small piece of yellowing paper.

Double letters

accelerate
accommodation
address
beginning
caterpillar
collector
disappear
embarrass
exaggerate
happiness

interrogate
kidnapped
mattress
miscellaneous
necessary
officer
passage
porridge
possess
professional

success
terrible
vacuum
woollen
wrapper

Awkward customers

argument
beautiful
breakfast
building
business
centre
chemist
cheque
chimney
cough
cousin
cupboard
dangerous
daughter
dictionary
disease
electricity
encyclopaedia
February

foreign
friend
gauge
government
guard
headache
height
hospital
humorous
island
knowledgeable
language
library
minute
neighbour
nephew
niece
orchestra
parliament

people
pigeon
queue
recipe
rhyme
saucer
scissors
separate
situated
special
usually
valley
vegetable
vehicle
vinegar
Wednesday
welcome
wheat

Acknowledgements

The publishers would like to thank the following for permission to reproduce photographs:

Ardea, pp. 29, 35, 127; Barnaby's Picture Library, p. 81; Camera Press, pp. 54, 74, 81, 85, 119, 131; Bruce Coleman p. 122; Rex Features Ltd., p. 81; Sally and Richard Greenhill, pp. 4, 23, 67, 103; Nick Hedges, p. 15; Eric Hosking, pp. 29, 35, 120; Keystone Press Agency, pp. 15, 26, 74, 81, 117, 136; Frank W. Lane, pp. 37, 59; Lawrence Lawry, pp. 140–1; Roger Mayne, p.6; Popperfoto, p. 83; W. Heath Robinson/Duckworth, p. 1; John Topham Picture Library, pp. 29, 35, 74

Illustrations by: Allan Curless, Jennifer Northway, Gary Rees, Malcolm Stokes, John Woodcock

Cover photograph courtesy of Photo Library International

The publishers would like to thank the following for permission to reprint copyright material:

Chester Aaron: from *An American Ghost*. © 1973 by Chester Aaron. Reprinted by permission of the author and A. P. Watt Ltd. Richard Adams: from *Watership Down* (Rex Collings). Reprinted by permission of David Higham Associates Ltd. Tachibana Akemi: from 'Poems of solitary delights' from *The Penguin Book of Japanese Verse*, trans. Geoffrey Bownas and Anthony Thwaite (The Penguin Poets, 1964) pp. 142–143. Copyright © Geoffrey Bownas and Anthony Thwaite, 1964. Reprinted by kind permission of Penguin Books Ltd. Stan Barstow: from *Joby*. Reprinted by permission of Michael Joseph Ltd. Nina Bawden: from *Squib*. Reprinted by permission of Victor Gollancz Ltd. Geoffrey Bowman: from *From Scott to Fuchs* (Frank C. Betts Ltd.). Geoffrey Bownas & Anthony Thwaite: *The Penguin Book of Japanese Verse* see Tachibana Akemi, and Tsuboi Shegeji. Ray Bradbury: from *The Illustrated Man*. Copyright © 1951 by Ray Bradbury, © renewed 1979 by Ray Bradbury. Reprinted by permission of the Harold Matson Company, Inc. *British Telecom* for permission to reproduce an extract from the telephone directory on how to call Emergency Services. Betsy Byars: from *The Eighteenth Emergency*. Reprinted by permission of the Bodley Head. Charles Causley: 'Millers End' from *Figgie Hobbin* (Macmillan). Reprinted by permission of David Higham Associates Ltd. Aidan Chambers: from *Funny Folk*. Reprinted by permission of William Heinemann Ltd. Arthur C. Clarke: from *Of Time and Stars* (Gollancz). Reprinted by permission of David Higham Associates Ltd. Angela Creese: from *Safety for your Family*. Reprinted by permission of Bell & Hyman Ltd. Roald Dahl: from *Charlie and the Chocolate Factory*. Reprinted by permission of George Allen & Unwin (Publishers) Ltd. Alan T. Dale: from *New World*. Copyright © OUP 1967. Reprinted by permission of Oxford University Press. Diagram Group: 'The hyena and the villagers', adapted from *The Way to Play* © Diagram Visual Information Ltd., New York. D. J. Enright: 'The Rebel' from *Rhyme Times Rhyme* (Chatto & Windus Ltd.). Reprinted by permission of Bolt & Watson Ltd., agents. Nicholas Fisk: from *Trillions*. Reprinted by permission of Hamish Hamilton Ltd. Robert Froman: 'Sudden Silence' and 'When Birds Remember', two concrete poems as art, from *Seeing Things*: A Book of Poems by Robert Froman, lettered by Ray Barber. Copyright © 1974 by Robert Froman. Reprinted by permission of Thomas Y. Crowell, Publishers. The poems as text are reprinted by permission of Abelard-Schuman Ltd, (The Blackie Publishing Group). Paul Gallico: from *The Snow Goose* (Michael Joseph). Reprinted by permission of Hughes Massie Ltd. Wilfred Gibson: 'Flannan Isle' from *Collected Poems*. Reprinted by permission of Michael Gibson and . Macmillan, London and Basingstoke. Rumer Godden: from *Diddakoi*. Reprinted by permission of Macmillan, London and Basingstoke. P. Haining: from *Ghosts: The Illustrated History*. Reprinted by permission of Sidgwick & Jackson. Gregory Harrison: 'The Weasel' from *Posting*

Letters (OUP). Copyright © 1968 Gregory Harrison. Reprinted by permission of the author. Florence Parry Heide: from *The Shrinking of Treehorn* (Puffin Books, 1975). Copyright © Florence Parry Heide, 1971. Reprinted by permission of Penguin Books Ltd. Russell Hoban: 'The Sparrowhawk' from *The Pedalling Man and other Poems*. Copyright © 1968. Published in the UK and British Commonwealth by World's Work Ltd., and reprinted with their permission. Elizabeth Jennings: 'Friends' from *The Secret Brother* (Macmillan). Reprinted by permission of David Higham Associates Ltd. W. E. Johns: from *Biggles Follows On*. Reprinted by permission of Hodder & Stoughton Ltd., (Children's Book division). James Kirkup: from *The Only Child* (Collins). Copyright © James Kirkup 1957. Reprinted by permission of Dr. Jan van Loewen Ltd., for the author. Gavin Maxwell: adapted from *The Rocks Remain* (Penguin Books, 1974). Copyright © Gavin Maxwell, 1963. Reprinted by permission of Penguin Books Ltd. Malcolm Muggeridge: from *Something Beautiful for God*. Reprinted by permission of Collins Publishers. Ogden Nash: 'The Ostrich' from *Collected Poems*. Reprinted by permission of A. P. Watt Ltd., for the Estate of Ogden Nash. Bill Naughton: from *The Goalkeeper's Revenge and Other Stories*. Reprinted by permission of George G. Harrap & Co. Ltd. *Oxford School Dictionary*: from 4th edition 1981 by permission of Oxford University Press. David Pelham: Adapted text and the Rogallo kite from p. 209 of *The Penguin Book of Kites* by David Pelham. Reproduced by permission of the author. Helen Rezatto: from an article which first appeared in *Southwest Review*, Spring 1963. Copyright 1963 by Southern Methodist University Press. Reprinted by permission. Michael Rosen : 'In the Daytime' and 'I'm alone in the evening' from *Mind Your Own Business*. Reprinted by permission of Andre Deutsch Ltd. Justin St. John: 'Hard Cheese' from *Junior Voices III*, ed. Geoffrey Summerfield (Penguin Education, 1970) pp. 68–70. This selection copyright © Geoffrey Summerfield 1970. Reprinted by permission of Penguin Books Ltd. Vernon Scannell: 'Hide and Seek' from *Walking Wounded* (Eyre & Spottiswoode). Reprinted by permission of the author. Ian Serraillier: Chapter 3 from *The Way of Danger* (pp. 12–19 of the OUP edition). Copyright © Ian Serraillier 1962. (New edition published by Heinemann Educational Books). Reprinted by permission of the author. Carl Sesar: *Poems to Eat* see Ishikawa Takuboku. Tsuboi Shigeji: 'Silent, but . . .' from *The Penguin Book of Japanese Verse*, trans. Geoffrey Bownas and Anthony Thwaite (The Penguin Poets 1964) p. 191. Copyright © Geoffrey Bownas and Anthony Thwaite, 1964. Reprinted by permission of Penguin Books Ltd. Noel Simon: Adapted from pp. 37–8 of *Lions*. Reprinted by permission of J. M. Dent & Sons Ltd. Armstrong Sperry: from *The Boy Who Was Afraid*. Reprinted by permission of The Bodley Head. Ishikawa Takuboku: 'Accidentally', trans. by Carl Sesar in *Poems to Eat* (Kodansha International Ltd.) Reprinted by permission of Carl Sesar. A. R. Taylor: from *Pub Games* (Mayflower). Reprinted by permission of Granada Publishing Ltd. Dylan Thomas: 'Enemies or Friends' from *Portrait of the Artist as a Young Dog* (J. M. Dent). Reprinted by permission of David Higham Associates Ltd. Flora Thompson: from *Lark Rise to Candleford* (1954). Reprinted by permission of Oxford University Press. Arthur Waley: 'The Red Cockatoo' by Po Chu-I trans. by Arthur Waley in *Chinese Poems*. Reprinted by permission of George Allen & Unwin (Publishers) Ltd. Philip Whitfield: Adapted from *The Hunters* (pp. 34–5). Reprinted by permission of The Hamlyn Publishing Group Ltd. Norman Wymer: adapted from *Medical Scientists and Doctors*. Copyright © OUP 1958. Reprinted by permission of Oxford University Press.

Every effort has been made to trace and contact copyright holders but this has not always been possible. We apologise for any infringement of copyright.

Oxford Secondary English is intended for use with pupils of a wide range of ability in the first three years of secondary schools.

Book 1 is organized in two parts. Section A is an illustrated anthology of fiction and fact, prose and poetry, arranged in nine thematic units, with word-study exercises, puzzles, and games at the end of each. Writing and discussion work is given at the beginning of each unit, but the teacher's book contains the majority of work assignments and these can be reproduced for class use.

Section A also contains three 'special' units. These present imaginary characters and situations, either fantastic or adventurous, which give scope for extended writing.

Section B contains explanations with exercises on language skills such as spelling, letter-writing, the form of sentences, punctuation, script-writing, and using a dictionary.

The other books in the *Oxford Secondary English* series are:

Teacher's Book 1   0 19 831134 6
Book 2   0 19 831135 4   *Teacher's Book 2*   0 19 831136 2
Book 3   0 19 831137 0   *Teacher's Book 3*   0 19 831138 9

ISBN 0 19 831133 8

Oxford University Press

ISBN 0-19-831133-8

9 780198 311331